Square One:
The Foundations
of Knowledge

Steve Patterson

To anyone seeking the truth.

Table of Contents

The Next Step   125

Introduction

Truth is discoverable. I'm certain of it. It's not popular to say. It's not popular to think. But I know it's true. Anybody can discover truth if they know where to look. It only requires skepticism and an open mind. Don't take my word for it. Scrutinize every claim in this book, and if you discover no truth, then you may confidently discard it in the trash.

The reader can rest assured: this book is not a work of academic philosophy. It's not incomprehensible or irrelevant. It doesn't try to sound profound by hiding behind opaque language. It is meant to be read and understood.

The first two chapters are preface. The core ideas are in Chapters Three and Four, and the last chapter is my response to anticipated objections. My conclusions are based on a decade of radical doubt and introspection. I was not sure if truth could be discovered, but now my extreme skepticism has been overcome, and I want to share the reasons why.

Chapter One:
Foundations

The Roots of a Tree

Every worldview is structured like a tree. Each part is connected to another part. Leaves are connected to branches. Branches are connected to the trunk. The trunk grows out of its roots.

The same is true for a worldview. The outermost part – the conclusions – are stuck to premises. Those premises are stuck to deeper premises, which ultimately grow out of their foundations. Leaves do not float in mid-air, and neither do our conclusions.

If you're looking at a particularly dense tree, it might be difficult to see past the leaves, but you can still know that branches lay underneath. Worldviews work the same way. Most people have a difficult time seeing past their conclusions to the premises that lay underneath. But if you care about the accuracy of your worldview, conclusions are largely irrelevant. They are at the end of a hierarchy.

Conclusions sprout from premises, and premises sprout from foundations.

If our premises are wrong, our conclusions will likely be wrong. If our foundations are wrong, our conclusions will be hopeless. Arriving at true conclusions with flawed foundations would be like winning a chess game against a Grandmaster without even understanding the rules. It's possible, but you'll probably lose in about ten moves.

Modern philosophy is dominated by schools of thought that deny the existence of foundations. They argue that worldviews aren't like trees; they are more like spider webs. Each part is connected together with no clear hierarchy of importance. Each thread is fallible and can be removed without destroying the whole structure.

In modern Western culture, it's fashionable to dismiss the search for foundations. It's seen as naïve and a waste of time – as if everyone already knows that foundations are indiscoverable.

I disagree. After searching for foundations, I've discovered them. Not only do they exist – they *necessarily* exist. They are *inescapable*, and given their importance, we'd better make sure they are accurate. If our most fundamental ideas about the world are wrong, then errors will permeate our entire worldview.

The Foundation of a House

Imagine you're trying to build a house. Where do you start? Well, you don't start building a house from the roof down. You don't install windows before the frame of the house has been erected. You don't paint the walls before the walls exist. There's a methodology – a hierarchy of importance. If the goal is to build a house that doesn't fall down, then its paint color is least important. The *foundation* is most important. It doesn't matter how ambitious your plans are, nor how pretty your interior design is. If you've built your house on a swamp, it will sink. Even if your house is a massive castle, if it's built on sand, it will crumble.

Worldviews are the same. The visible conclusions are like paint color and window dressings. They are largely irrelevant. The most important parts are the framework and foundations – the core structural parts. Most people get distracted by their conclusions while their foundations remain unexamined. Imagine trying to judge the sturdiness of a house by looking at its paint color. That's akin to people trying to judge the soundness of a worldview by looking at its conclusions.

Unfortunately, once a worldview is already built, the most fundamental ideas become the most difficult to change. A flawed foundation is much easier to ignore than to revise. Many people think that foundations aren't even worth investigating, because they assume *others* have already sorted them out. I think this is a mistake.

I suggest examining the foundations for yourself. If you don't want a house that collapses at the slightest breeze, or a worldview that collapses under the slightest examination, then it's up to you to investigate and lay your own foundations.

Rotten Wood

The actual process of getting to foundations is difficult, both practically and psychologically. We have to find a reliable method for sorting through our own ideas, and then we have to accept the pain of being wrong – fundamentally wrong, about the most basic ideas in our worldview. This process of self-examination involves large amounts of doubt, discomfort, and revision.

The doubt must be universal. You have to doubt yourself, your peers, professors, pastors, parents. Everybody. Trusting other people serves no purpose when searching for the premises and foundations of a worldview. In fact, it can be counterproductive. When you trust other people, you outsource your critical thinking to somebody else. That creates room for error. If someone makes a mistake, but their claims aren't investigated because you trust them, that mistake will never be corrected. Trust might be practical for day-to-day living, but for serious intellectual investigation, it's a big mistake.

Self-doubt can be especially unsettling. If you've never examined the premises for your beliefs, there's no good reason to think they are true – and no good reason to think the conclusions that follow are true either. Self-doubt can create a domino effect, resulting in the destruction of a significant part of your worldview. To use the tree analogy, when you chop away at a tree's limbs, the smaller branches and leaves fall to the ground. When you chop at the trunk and roots, the entire tree might come crashing down. The longer a tree grows unhampered, the bigger it will be and the more difficult to cut down. The longer a worldview goes unexamined, the more difficult it becomes to revise. People who have committed themselves to an idea for decades – basing their personal values, career, or life decisions on it – will have a difficult time accepting that their most fundamental ideas about the world are wrong. The psychological stakes are too high for such a revision. It's much easier to simply overlook errors and keep your worldview together.

Take a concrete example: astrology. Let's say somebody has studied astrology for thirty years. They've amassed a huge amount of knowledge. They know the various theories and histories, and they have a large, passionate community of fellow astrologers who all share the same assumptions about how the world works.

We don't usually think of it, but astrologers have a theory with explanatory power. They have reasons for their beliefs. The reason that so many Leos are extroverts, they say, is because there's a connection between people's disposition and their birth sign. Now, that's *not a very good* explanation, but it's still an explanation. If an astrologer seeks out confirmation for his theory, he'll find it. There are extroverted Leos everywhere. If he isn't interested in alternative theoretical explanations, he will have little reason to change his beliefs.

However, let's say, for some reason, an astrologer gets skeptical. He starts to doubt his own premises. Imagine he investigates the fundamental connection between the stars and Earth and concludes, "The position of the stars does *not* influence human disposition after all." He'd been making a consistent, fundamental error for decades. The error is foundational to astrological theory, and an entire structure of knowledge rests upon it. What can he do?

The easiest thing would be to ignore the error so that it doesn't cause discomfort. To cease thinking about it. The next easiest thing would be to acknowledge the error but deny its importance. He could think, "Yeah, the connection between stars and humans is probably mistaken, but whatever. It doesn't matter. It's only one idea, and the rest of the theory makes so much sense. I'm not going to throw out the whole thing because of one issue. Horoscopes still help me explain the world." Or, he could do the most difficult thing: reject the entire structure of knowledge built on top of flawed foundations. He could reject the conclusions of astrology since the premises contain a fundamental flaw. He could admit that his thirty years of study were largely a waste of time.

From my experience, I think the last option is the least likely for people to choose. It's too embarrassing and unsettling, and it requires restarting an intellectual journey from scratch. However, this option is my suggestion for anybody seeking the truth. It doesn't matter how elaborate or beautiful a theory is. It doesn't matter how long you've believed it. If it's foundationally mistaken, it should be discarded. If the roots are rotten, the tree is dead, and it's best to let the entire thing collapse.

Such a radical revision is easier said than done. Fortunately, powerful tools exist to help anyone critically examine and revise their own worldview. It starts with a mindset: skepticism. Radical, intense, and uncomfortable skepticism.

Skepticism

Imagine your neighbor comes up to you and says, "I just bought $100 trillion worth of property in Montana!" Would you believe him? I suspect you'd feel a bit skeptical. $100 trillion is a lot of money – five times more than the US national debt.

That suspicious feeling in your mind – smelling that something is fishy – is the correct mindset for critical thinking. Call it "skepticism." Skepticism helps us cut through the rotten wood in a worldview. It helps us get down to the foundations. Skepticism should be directed at everybody, including yourself. That means challenging and doubting every single idea you encounter. Assume that every idea is fishy, even if you don't smell it yet. Such extreme skepticism is easily justified. After all:

(1) Foundations are categorically more important than conclusions.
(2) Most people never examine their foundations.
(3) Therefore, most people do not deeply understand their own ideas and should not be trusted.

For simplicity's sake, I suggest this starting point: assume everything you believe, everything you've heard, and everything other people believe is wrong. Start from scratch, and see if any knowledge can fully withstand an onslaught of skeptical reasoning. If *certain* truth exists – knowledge which cannot possibly be wrong – then that can serve as a trustworthy foundation for the rest of our worldview. If certain knowledge doesn't exist, then we must accept the fact that our belief systems are without ultimate justification, and we're stuck only with best-guesses.

When constructing a house, it's best to remove all the sand and loose earth from the spot that you want to build on. You need a solid foundation to be confident that your house won't suddenly collapse underneath you.

This book is about the search for solid foundations – certain truths on which to build your worldview. After searching, I've discovered them. Certain foundations are both *necessary* and *inescapable*. I will explain these qualities in Chapter Three.

The skeptical mindset is essential for finding truth, but it can also become dogmatic. Extreme skeptics will unwittingly contradict themselves by claiming, "I am certain that certain knowledge doesn't exist!" Skepticism, in order to be consistent, must be applied to itself. To insist that "Truth cannot be known!", regardless of the evidence, is equally as dogmatic as insisting that, "All my beliefs are absolute truth!" without evidence. Certain knowledge might exist, or it might not. The careful skeptic must not close his mind to either possibility.

From Top to Bottom

An excellent tool for going from conclusions to premises, then from premises to foundations, is a question: "why?" It doesn't matter the starting idea. Ask "why?" a few times in a row, and you'll quickly get into foundational issues. For example, take the sentence:

(1)   I am sitting on a chair.

For most people, this seems so obvious that it doesn't warrant inspection. Isn't it self-evident whether or not I'm sitting on a chair? Well, let's ask the question. *Why* do I believe I'm sitting on a chair?

Answer: I feel it beneath me. For most people, this is sufficient reason to believe, and it's usually the end of an inquiry. But for our purposes, we need to go deeper. *Why* do I think I feel a chair beneath me?

This is a more difficult question to answer. I feel something, but why do I believe it's a chair? Perhaps I don't actually feel "a chair beneath me," and I am simply feeling my feelings *that I assume come from a chair?* I mean, it's entirely possible that I'm hallucinating right now. I *think* I'm feeling a chair, but in reality, it could be an illusion. I could be feeling my feelings without those feelings coming from a chair. So then why do I assume that my feelings correlate with any external world at all? Why do I think I'm not hallucinating?

These are not easy questions, and philosophers have been debating them for thousands of years. It only took a handful of "why?" questions to get down to some very murky issues.

If we want to discover the truth, we shouldn't waste time arguing at the surface level – about "whether or not I'm sitting on a chair." We have to go deeper. We have to sort out whether our feelings correspond to an external world. We need to grapple with the possibility of hallucinations. After the foundations have been sorted, then perhaps the original question can be answered.

Intuitively, it seems like "why?" questions can be asked without end – that ideas cannot stand alone without deeper reasons. But in fact, there are truths so foundational that the question "why?" does not apply. These truths are not contingent on other premises; they are necessary. In fact, these truths are so fundamental, that every other idea presupposes them. They rest at the bottom of every worldview, whether explicit or implicit. They are certain, absolute, and objective. Without them, one cannot even have coherent thoughts.

To return to the tree and building analogies: Ultimately, every tree shares the same roots. Every building is built on the same bedrock foundation. If we desire to have an accurate worldview, such truths are immensely important.

Chapter Two:
Implausible and Impossible

Two Types of Argument

Claiming that "I've discovered objective, certain truth!" is controversial in both philosophic and non-philosophic circles. So before explaining, I want to first categorize some standard, skeptical objections. There are two types of arguments against certain knowledge – arguments from *implausibility* and arguments from *impossibility*.

The arguments from implausibility claim that it's extremely unlikely – though theoretically possible – that humans could have access to certain knowledge. The chances are so low that the skeptics think it's unreasonable or naive to claim certainty about anything.

The arguments from impossibility claim that it's *impossible in principle* to know anything with certainty – due to the incomprehensible structure of the universe, the flaws in human reasoning, or logical paradoxes that cannot be resolved.

The implausibility and impossibility arguments have many versions, and I will address them separately. Chapter Two will cover implausibility. Chapter Five will cover impossibility. They are split up for a simple reason. All that's required to refute the arguments from implausibility is one demonstration of a certain truth. Since several certain truths will be demonstrated in Chapter Three, the implausibility arguments will be refuted as a group. However, these demonstrations will not satisfy people who make arguments from impossibility. Their arguments are more complex and will require additional elaboration. In almost every case, the arguments from impossibility are based on an incorrect use of language, and they will be addressed individually in Chapter Five.

So, the rest of this chapter will be devoted to seven common arguments for the implausibility of certain truth. These arguments won't be deeply sophisticated – just summarized positions of popular ideas.

Mistaken Humility

Perhaps the most popular argument from implausibility goes like this: Humans are fallible. We make mistakes all the time. Even if we're convinced that we're correct in the present, we cannot know what information we'll have in the future. So we shouldn't be certain about anything, because that would close our minds to the possibility of error. Certainty enables dogmatism. Furthermore, experts and intellectuals disagree all the time about everything, and even the best ideas are constantly being proven wrong. What seems certainly true now might be certainly false in the future. Therefore, all propositions should be treated as empirical hypotheses, always ready to be revised with additional data. That's a more scientific approach to knowledge.

The argument often continues: Truth-seeking must be a communal endeavor because each individual person has too limited a perspective. "Certain truth" would be equivalent to "the one opinion that is objectively true for all time, regardless of whether everybody disagrees." But such a claim seems naïve. It's unrealistic to think that one person/group could have access to absolute truth if the rest of the world disagrees with them. Therefore, humans are never justified in believing any kind of "absolute knowledge" or "certain truth."

On the surface, this argument seems reasonable. Arrogance and overconfidence can surely cloud one's critical thinking. Listening to others and trusting their analyses keeps our own intellectual egos in check. Indeed, being rational requires a willingness to be proven wrong. But it can be taken too far.

Dogmatic thinking should be avoided, but *insisting that all knowledge is uncertain* is itself dogmatic. To keep a truly open mind, one must entertain the possibility that certain truth exists. Maybe it does; maybe it doesn't. We can't rule it out before investigation.

No Land Across the Sea

Another popular argument is about simple odds. People think that in order to have certain knowledge, you must amass a gigantic amount of information – more than one person can realistically accumulate in a lifetime. Or, they think that the total amount of certain knowledge is so tiny that you'll never be able to discover any. Searching for it is like a hopeless crusade to find a diamond that's buried somewhere in the Sahara. Essentially, it's a complete waste of time.

These arguments make me think of early Europeans who had never crossed the Atlantic. I'm sure they wondered whether there was land across the ocean. If they never crossed, or if they never met anybody who crossed, it's easy to understand why they would feel confident declaring, "There's no land across the ocean! It's just water the whole way!" Or perhaps in a more open-minded way, "*Maybe* you'll find a small island in the ocean, but because there's so much water, the chances are tiny!" To back up their claims, they might have even sailed out on their own boats for miles and miles. Water as far as the eye can see. Therefore they conclude, "There's nothing out there. It's water forever, and it's a hopeless crusade to think you'll find land." If nobody ever crossed and came back, they would have no reason to believe otherwise.

Of course, we know there is land across the Atlantic, and it's not a small island. To discover it, you have to be willing to sail far enough out into the ocean. You also have to be willing to entertain the ridicule from those who have never crossed before and are convinced it's a hopeless project.

The same is true when searching for certain, foundational knowledge. Skeptics prematurely conclude that certain truth doesn't exist, or that if it does, we'll never know about it. They think we're drifting in an endless sea of uncertainty. But that's because they haven't ventured far enough into the water.

Faith in Something

Another common objection is the argument from faith. Growing up in a Christian Evangelical household, I am personally familiar with this one. Religious people often claim that no worldview can be rationally justified down to its foundations, because at some point, the rationality stops, and we're left with sheer faith.

They'll often say, "You can't *ultimately* know what you believe is true. You have to have faith *in something*. You just have faith in your own rational faculties!" Of course, this is usually followed by, "And since faith is inescapable, you should have faith in my specific deity."

Their argument brings a visual to mind: a gigantic castle whose base is surrounded by clouds. The castle represents an impressive, consistent, and intricate theology. The clouds are a barrier preventing the examination of the theology's foundations. If you focus on the stone towers, ornate tapestry, and external beauty of the castle, you'll be convinced it's rock-solid. However, if you search for the foundations, you might become skeptical. The inhabitants of the castle don't see a problem. They don't bother examining their foundations and are convinced that all structures are built the same way – impressive towers built on top of impenetrable fog.

We're supposed to believe that worldviews work the same way. Conclusions are built on premises; premises are built on deeper premises; but the deepest foundations always elude our rational analysis. We must simply hope that they are true.

All that would be required to refute the argument from faith is a demonstration of one certain truth. If certainty can be discovered, it would demonstrate that the inhabitants of the castle are wrong. The fog isn't impenetrable. Their castle does have examinable foundations – it's built on top of a swamp.

As this book will demonstrate, you don't have to have faith in anything. You can be rational all the way down to your foundations.

The Evolved Brain

Another objection comes from human biology. Think about the brain. It's a chunk of meat inside the skull of a mammal. Why should we think that such an object would have access to certain truth? The human brain has evolved for a reason: to effectively navigate the world for successful procreation. That's a very different reason than "to grasp true insights into the nature of the universe."

From this perspective, our beliefs about the world aren't about what's objectively true. Rather, they are about *what works*. We have no reason to believe that brains can grasp certain truth when they are hardwired for navigation and procreation.

Along these lines, people often claim that what is required to know something with absolute certainty is the ability to "get outside our own minds" to verify things from an objective point of view – the so-called "God's eye perspective." Humans cannot do this. We are stuck inside our own subjective perspective, and therefore, we cannot claim anything with certainty. We are only left with best-guesses.

These arguments make a good point. It seems implausible to think that the mammalian brain could have access to certain truth. Humans are limited creatures. However, just because something is implausible doesn't mean we can rule it out. It remains an open question.

A Senseless Universe

Another similar objection has to do with the nature of the universe itself. The argument goes: Humans mistakenly assume that the universe is comprehensible. We have no reason to believe this is true. The universe isn't somehow bound by rules of human rationality. Nature doesn't care about making sense to us. When we claim to find truth, we're simply projecting an artificial orderliness onto something non-orderly. Nature might be chaotic and senseless, with our minds simply picking patterns out of the chaos. It's like we're playing connect-the-dots with static on a television screen. We're just making stuff up. Therefore, if the universe is incomprehensible to humans, the pursuit of truth is a vain project. We cannot comprehend what cannot be comprehended.

This argument makes an interesting point. It does seem odd that something so enormous and complex as the universe should make sense to small and simple humans. However, just because something is odd doesn't mean it's impossible. If we can make sense of *anything*, then we can make sense of some part of the universe. All it would take is one empirical demonstration of a certain truth.

Language is Imprecise

Other people point to the limits of language as the reason humans cannot know anything with certainty. The argument goes: Words do not have objective meaning. Everybody uses words a bit differently. Therefore, it doesn't really make sense to say, "We can know objective, certain truth." Language is too imprecise for that. The words "objective," "certain," and "truth" mean different things to different people. What might appear "true" to me, might not be "true" to you, because we do not share a common definition for "true."

This argument slightly misses the issue. While it's true that *communication* might be imprecise, it doesn't follow that our own personal concepts cannot be precise. We might not be able to express ourselves clearly, but that doesn't mean we can't understand things clearly.

Communication, by its nature, is a public act. It requires multiple people. By contrast, discovering truth is a solo endeavor. You can only evaluate concepts within your own mind. You can't peer into the mind of somebody else. Even when somebody communicates with you, they aren't somehow placing their concepts directly into your mind for evaluation. They are using words to spark the generation of concepts *in your mind, by your mind*.

So it's a mistake to focus on the linguistic definitions for words. Truth seeking isn't about having "objectively correct definitions" that can be communicated to other people. It's about analyzing the concepts that are generated in your own mind by the words you read. Whether or not there has been precise communication is irrelevant. My assumption is that, if you're reading this, we speak the same language, and therefore the concepts you will be evaluating will be similar to the concepts I wish to communicate.

However, even if I'm the only person who understands the meaning of my words, it's still possible that those words correspond to reality. The question of certain truth is about *rational, individual comprehension*, not effective communication.

Sense-Perception

The final argument from implausibility has to do with our senses. Philosophers and skeptics have been talking about this idea for millennia. The argument goes: Our senses are not trustworthy. They frequently deceive us. What seems self-evidently true might turn out to be illusory. Therefore, we cannot have certainty about anything.

For example, place a pencil in a glass of water, and it appears bent. Look all you want, from any angle, and your eyes will lie to you. The pencil isn't actually bent. Or, take something as mundane as watching a movie. Your visual experience is smooth and continuous – the images look like they blend together seamlessly. However, this is an illusion. Most films are shot at around thirty frames per second. That means you're actually looking at thirty static images played in rapid succession every second. Your brain tricks you into thinking you're seeing continuous motion; in reality, it's jumpy and broken.

Take a more obvious example: hallucinations. Since the beginning of history, humans have been seeing things that aren't there. Their senses deceive them, whether it's seeing an oasis in a desert, a goblin in a cave, or a talking elephant after they've ingested drugs.

These are simple examples, but they illustrate the point that we cannot blindly trust our senses. If our senses trick us some of the time, couldn't they be tricking us all the time? Couldn't we simply be hallucinating all day, every day? It's at least possible. If our senses are indeed tricking us, or if we're constantly hallucinating, then we cannot claim we know anything with certainty.

I am sympathetic to this argument. People do place far too much trust in their senses. However, even if we're constantly hallucinating and only see illusions, it doesn't exclude the possibility of certain knowledge. The reason is because *some ideas are independent of our senses*. We can have knowledge which is true regardless of sensory input, and in fact, it's this kind of knowledge that underpins the rest of our worldview.

Simple Refutation

All seven of these arguments agree on the same core idea: certain truth might exist, but we'll probably never know about it, and if we're being realistic, certainty is beyond the reach of humans. The next two chapters will refute the arguments from implausibility *in kind*. Several certain truths will be demonstrated.

Before doing so, I want to caution the reader. The demonstrations of certain truth are simple, self-evident, and anti-climatic. If you have a strong intuition or common sense, your reaction will be "Of course! This is so obvious!" That is a good reaction, but realize that every point is passionately objected to by skeptics.

Several certain truths will be demonstrated, explained, then restated multiple ways. The purpose of this is to remove any shadow of a doubt, regardless of the reader's background in philosophy. Given the importance of the subject, a thorough explanation of what is self-evidently true is required.

Chapter Three:
Logic and Existence

Increasing Confidence

Most ideas are not certainly true. They fall onto a spectrum. Instead of being pure black or white, they are various shades of gray. To understand the certain truths – those on the outermost ends of the spectrum – it helps to first analyze the less-than-certain ideas in the middle. Let's start with the proposition:

(1) More people live in the United States than in Australia.

Most people, if they have some understanding of geography, history, or demographics will believe this is a true statement. It's estimated that around 325 million people live in the United States, and around 25 million people live in Australia. It seems reasonable to believe that proposition 1 is true. But can we be certain?

No, we cannot. It takes just a little imagination to see why. First of all, nobody has ever actually counted up the people living in the United States and Australia. They use rough guesses. Perhaps the criteria they use to approximate population are flawed. That's possible. Or perhaps there's a gigantic underground civilization in Australia that's never been discovered. Or perhaps a biological weapon was just released a few hours ago in the United States, killing hundreds of millions of people. If that's the case, then there could be more people living in Australia right now. It's not likely, but it's possible. We cannot be certain. Consider another proposition:

> (2) If a hammer is dropped from a building, it will fall towards the earth.

I feel much more confident about this one. While I may never have counted the people living in Australia, I have dropped plenty of things, and they all fall down. Everybody that I've spoken to has reported the same experience. In fact, it's probably true to say that *every* hammer dropped from a building has *always* fallen towards the earth. Does that mean we've discovered a certain truth?

No, it doesn't. We can imagine many circumstances in which the hammer might not fall down. Therefore, we cannot be certain. For example, imagine the hammer was dropped on top of a rocket. The moment it was let go, the rocket made contact and pushed the hammer all the way into outer space, escaping the earth's orbit. In that case, it might fall towards Jupiter instead. Ridiculous scenario? Yes. But is it conceivably possible? Of course.

Now imagine there was no rocket. You let go of the hammer, and it floats in front of you. You didn't know beforehand that the laws of physics change every 10,000 years. You just so happened to have dropped the hammer at the moment the laws of physics changed. Now, instead of falling, hammers float in mid-air. Is it possible? Of course. And there's no way you could figure it out before-hand. If the laws of physics change every 10,000 years, then the last time it happened was before recorded history, so you couldn't have possibly known about it. Not even the laws of gravity are certain. Let's go one step further. Examine the next proposition:

(3) Hands are attached to the end of my arms.

Can I be sure of this? I'm looking at my hands, and sure enough, they are attached to my arms. Unfortunately, that is not sufficient criteria for certain knowledge. It is conceivably possible that I am mistaken. What if, unbeknownst to me, somebody secretly placed hallucinogenic mushrooms in my breakfast this morning. Then, once I started hallucinating, they cut off my hands without me being aware of it. When I look down, I see hands, but they could be an illusion. Perhaps once I sober up, I'll realize I am handless. (Though, admittedly, it would be hard to type this book without hands. Perhaps that experience, too, is an illusion.)

Or perhaps I'm stuck in a deep sleep. I might be dreaming that I have hands, when in reality, I am some Martian whose body is a gelatinous blob. The dream might have lasted for so long that I've forgotten I'm asleep. Is it possible? Yes. Do I believe I am a gelatinous blob stuck in a dream? No. But I cannot claim certainty. Now consider a different type of proposition:

(4)   All students with blonde hair are students.

Think about it. Is this certainly true? In some bizarre circumstance, could a student with blonde hair not be a student? Use your imagination. I think you'll discover that this is a certainly true proposition if we're precise with the meaning of our words. There is no scenario in which a student with blonde hair could not be a student. Not even in a dream. Not even if the laws of physics were different.

Now, somebody might object, "What if we *think* somebody is a student with blonde hair, but it turns out they aren't really a student?" Well, such a circumstance does not change the truth of the proposition. If somebody isn't really a student, then they aren't really a student with blonde hair. If somebody is actually a student with blonde hair, then they must be a student. A *necessary* criterion for "being a student with blonde hair" is "being a student" in the first place. Consider another example:

(5) There are no married bachelors.

Think about it. If "bachelor" means "unmarried man," are there any married men who are unmarried? Could there ever be such a thing? I'd say no. There could never be a married man who is unmarried. If he were unmarried, then he wouldn't be married in the first place. You can be certain of it. This is true in all possible universes. It's true on Mars. It's true if we're hallucinating. In all cases when a man is married, he is married.

It isn't an empirical hypothesis whether or not married bachelors exist. You don't have to go out and run experiments in the world. It can be understood simply by grasping the meaning of our words. Consider one final example:

(6) If Fido is a dog, then he is a dog.

This is also certainly true. In no possible scenario could Fido be a dog and not a dog at the same time. You don't have to wonder whether, in some weird case, Fido could be a dog-that-isn't-a-dog. All dogs are dogs. No dogs are not dogs. If anything is a dog, then it must be a dog, and it must not be a non-dog. These are certain truths.

Propositions 1, 2, and 3 are different *in kind* from propositions 4, 5, and 6. There's a reason for that. The latter three propositions are certain truths, but they do not represent the foundations of knowledge. They are not square one. We have to go one step deeper.

Logic

We need to ask "why?" a few more times. Why are certain propositions certain? Why are there no married bachelors? Why are all dogs, dogs? The intuitive answer is to say, "It's just got to be that way!" That is true. It does have to be that way, but that doesn't explain why. The answer is:

Logic.

Logic is the reason that bachelors cannot be married. It's the reason that dogs are dogs. It's also the reason that 2 + 2 = 4. Logic can be understood as *the rules of existence*. All propositions, regardless of their content, presuppose the same rules of existence. These rules are not optional; they are *inescapable*, as I will explain.

Logic is where *necessity* comes from. When we say, "It's necessarily true that circles aren't square," we are appealing to logic. Logic is at the root of every philosophical tree. It's the foundation underpinning every worldview. It's presupposed by every sentence and every thought, whether realized or not. There are no exceptions to the rules, and we can be certain of it.

But don't take my word for it. By asking two more "why?" questions, we can get to the very bottom it all and the whole point of this book. *Why* is logic necessary, and *why* are there no exceptions? The answer is square one, the ultimate foundation of knowledge:

Logic and existence are inseparable.

This idea is important enough to rephrase many ways, at the risk of being repetitive. The following statements might appear as self-evident truisms, but when understood, they illustrate the most fundamental truth in philosophy:

> There is no non-logical type of existence, because in every case of existence, you have existence.

> There is no existent thing that is non-existent. Nothing exists which does not exist.

> A non-logical existence would be non-existence – and therefore, does not exist.

> If something does exist, it doesn't not-exist.

> Everything that exists, exists.

This means *logic applies to every existent thing by virtue of the fact that the thing exists and doesn't not-exist.* This is true for any type of existents, at any time, in any possible universe. We can know, with certainty, the most fundamental quality of any existent thing: that it exists – because if it didn't exist, it wouldn't exist, and therefore wouldn't be an existent thing.

For the philosophers reading, I am claiming that, at the very bottom of everything, epistemology and metaphysics blend together. We know knowledge because existents exist. This knowledge is not hypothetical. It isn't an empirical question or open to future revision. It can be understood simply by analyzing the meaning of the term "existent." No information – no additional data – could ever change "an existing existent" into "a non-existing existent." We can be sure of it.

These truths might seem obvious and repetitive. However, since they are not universally accepted, and since they are the most foundational ideas in philosophy, I intend to beat them to death, so that no reasonable person could disagree. The rest of this chapter is devoted to further examples and explanation.

Somebody familiar with these types of propositions might say, "These are just tautologies!" but this misses the point and conflates the *structure* of propositions with the *content* of propositions. The purpose of this book is to discover truth, regardless of the structure of the propositions which communicate that truth. The tautology objection is addressed in detail in Chapter Five.

There is no "escaping" logic. There is no "transcending" logic. The rules are inescapable for all existent things. You might say: to escape logic is to escape existence. The rules of existence do not apply to non-existence. Since no thing is non-existent, logic applies to everything.

Existence

I've used words like "existence," "existent," and "exist" without defining the terms. Here's what I mean.

To exist is to be.

"Existing" is *being*.

"An existent" is a thing that *is*.

Language is not a perfectly precise tool for communication, so I will try to reference this quality of "existing" in several ways.

A simple way to grasp the nature of existence is to analyze the difference between the eyeballs in your head and the eyeballs in your knee. One of those things has a property that the other lacks. That's *existence*. The eyeball in your head is an existent. The eyeball in your knee is not an existent.

When I look out the window, I see three small birds pecking at the grass. Assuming I'm not hallucinating, those birds *exist*. They *are*. Each one is an existent.

What about the elephant outside my window? Well, there exists no such thing. It *isn't*, and this is where language gets tricky. Imagine I were to ask, "If the elephant does not exist, then what are we referencing when we talk about it? How can we talk about a non-existent thing?"

In some sense, it is true that "if we're talking about a thing, it must exist." An essential part of "being a thing" is *being* in the first place. However, we have to distinguish between different types of existence. There is a difference between conceptual and non-conceptual existence – between dependent and independent existence.

"The elephant outside my window" is a concept. When we're talking about "it," we're talking about an idea. *The idea exists*, but its existence is dependent on my conceptualization of it. If nobody thought of "the elephant outside my window," it would have no type of existence.

The birds, on the other hand, are not concepts. They exist independent of our minds. If nobody were to think of them, they would still exist. We can conceive *of* the birds – and indeed, when we use the term "birds," we are referencing our conception of them. But those conceptions have *external referents*. The idea of the birds is different from the birds themselves.

"The elephant outside my window" is not different from "the idea of the elephant outside my window." That idea does not have an external referent. The same is true for "the eyeballs inside my knee." That concept does not refer to any independent thing.

To be precise: There exists no such thing as "the external referents that 'the eyeballs in your knee' refers to.'" There does exist such a thing as "the external referents that 'the birds outside my window' refers to." That distinction points at the meaning of the term "existing."

You'll notice that I've smuggled in an assumption here – that indeed, the birds do exist separate of my conception of them. How do I know this? Well, I don't know with certainty. It's an assumption, and it's a larger topic in the philosophy of language and metaphysics which is beyond the scope of this book. Things *might* exist outside of our minds, and the purpose of these examples was to illustrate the meaning of the term "exist," not to make the case for a mind-independent reality.

Identity

Existents must follow the rules of existence – what I call "logic." These rules have been written about for thousands of years, and they have been called different things. They've been called "the laws of thought," "the laws of language," "the rules of Reason," among other labels.

I prefer calling them "the rules of existence" because they do not only apply to thought, language, and rationality. They apply to every existent thing. So, for the rest of the book, I will be using the terms "laws of logic," "rules of existence," and "logic" interchangeably.

The most famous formalization of these rules comes from Aristotle, who coined three laws of logic:

(1) The law of identity.

(2) The law of non-contradiction.

(3) The law of the excluded middle.

I will be focusing on the first two. The law of identity says that "everything is identical with itself." In other words, things are what they are. They have whatever properties they have. A thing isn't more-than-itself or less-than-itself; it is precisely itself. It doesn't matter what the thing is or where it's located. This is a certain truth, and we can reference it another way. We can use abstract place-holders instead of concretes by saying "A is A." It doesn't matter what terms we substitute for "A." It could mean "Cathy is Cathy," "grass is grass," or anything else. Whatever "A" is, it is itself.

Every thing has identity. Every thing is something. No thing can exist without being something. To deny identity is to deny existence – to not be something. No thing can exist without being what it is.

Non-contradiction

The law of identity is equally as fundamental as the law of non-contradiction. Each law implies – and is ultimately a re-statement of – the other. The law of non-contradiction can be phrased as, "Things are not the way that they are not." In abstract form, "It is not the case that A and not-A."

Things cannot *be and not be* at the same time. They cannot have a property and not have that property at the same time. If something is some way, it isn't *not* that way. This is certainly true.

A contradiction is to claim "A and not-A" at the same time, in the same way. For example, I've contradicted myself if I claim that "I am six feet tall and I am not six feet tall." Or, "Joey is a human and Joey is not a human." Or, "Squares have four corners and squares do not have four corners." Contradictions make an assertion and its negation at the same time. They cannot be true, and they cannot exist. It isn't a hypothetical question, and it will become obvious as we examine the meaning of our words.

However, because of the imprecision of language, plenty of *apparent* contradictions exist. But in each case, additional clarity resolves the contradiction. For example, imagine I were to say, "I am tall and I am not tall." That sounds like a contradiction. However, I could explain, "Compared to the general public, I am tall. Compared to professional basketball players, I am not tall. Therefore, I am tall and not tall at the same time." But this is no contradiction. It's just a poorly constructed proposition hiding behind ambiguous words.

Contradictions take the form, "A and not-A." The tallness example is of the form "A and not-B." The claim is actually, "I am tall in some circumstances, and *in different circumstances,* I am not tall." No contradiction present. Contradictions must explicitly negate the proposition being affirmed. In this case, we could create a contradiction by saying, "I am tall in some circumstances, and in those same circumstances, it is not the case that I am tall." That's a proper contradiction, and it's certainly false. If I am tall in some circumstances, then I am tall in those circumstances.

The law of non-contradiction is simply restating the law of identity – things are the way that they are, and by extension, they are not the way that they are not.

Contradictions are *denials of identity*. Therefore, they are denials of existence. Contradictions do not exist because they *cannot* exist. Another way to understand:

(1) To exist is *to be.*

(2) To be is *to be some way.*

(3) Contradictions are a denial of being some way.

(4) Therefore, contradictions are a *denial of being.*

Therefore, in whatever way that something exists, its existence must be non-contradictory. It is whatever way that it is. To claim that "Something in the universe is contradictory" is to claim that "Something in the universe is not what it is." Or that "it is what it isn't." Claiming such a thing is a demonstration of confusion. It's like a man insisting, "It is impossible to attempt communication!" He doesn't understand the meaning of his words. If he did, he would realize that he had just attempted communication.

Inseparability

Logic and existence cannot be separated from one another. Logic isn't a property of existence, nor is existence a property of logic. There is no "non-logical part of existence," and there exists no "logical part of non-existence." Existence without logic would be existence without existence – i.e. non-existent.

No thing can exist without existing. Therefore, to the extent that existence exists, it is necessarily logical. Another way to understand this is by returning to the laws of identity and non-contradiction.

(1) You cannot have existence without identity.
(2) You cannot have identity without non-contradiction.

(3) Therefore, you cannot have existence without non-contradiction.

Putting 1 and 3 together: you cannot have existence without identity and non-contradiction – the two foundational laws of logic.

True and False

The laws of logic immediately imply two more concepts: truth and falsehood. The word "truth" can be ambiguous, so to avoid confusion, we must distinguish between "metaphysical truth" and "linguistic truth."

Metaphysical truth is simply *the way that things actually are.* You might say, "When we want to know the truth, we want to know the way things actually are."

Linguistic truth is about the relationship between language and reality. It's about words and the world. If a proposition claims that "X is the way that things are," and X is actually the way things are in the world, then that proposition is "true." If a proposition claims that "X is the way things are," and X is actually not the way things are in the world, then that proposition is "false." For example, if I claim that "There are three birds outside my window," and there are actually three birds outside my window, then that proposition is true. If there aren't actually three birds outside my window, then the claim "there are three birds outside my window" is false.

Linguistic truth does not make sense without metaphysical truth. True propositions tell us the truth about the world – otherwise, they wouldn't be true propositions. "Truth" isn't some arbitrary label that we assign to sentences. It comes from corresponding to the world outside of our language.

Notice the relationship between true and false. If something is true, then it isn't false. And if something is false, then it isn't true. This allows us to stack truth and falsehood claims on top of each other. For example, if there are not three birds outside my window, I could also say, "It is false *that it is true* that there are three birds outside my window." This would be a true statement.

In fact, an excellent technique to get closer to truth is by first discovering what is false. Every time you rule out something false, you inch closer to the truth by the process of elimination. And if you know something is false with certainty, you can know its negation is true with certainty.

Truth and falsehood are inseparably linked. You cannot understand the meaning of "false" without understanding the meaning of "true." You cannot have a true proposition that is false; you cannot have a false proposition that is true. That's what we mean by the terms.

Truth and falsehood follow directly from the laws of logic. If A is A, then it's true to say "A is A." If it's true that A is A, then it is false to claim that "'A is A' is false."

Logic, existence, truth, and falsehood are all necessarily bundled together. To the extent you have existence, you have existence, which means you have logic, which implies that any proposition claiming that "existents exist" is true, and any proposition claiming that "existents do not exist" is false. Without logic, the words "truth" and "falsehood" become meaningless – as what's true could be false, and what's not true could be true. If at any point, what's true is not true, then the word "true" becomes incoherent.

Negation

We can better understand the laws of logic by closely examining our own concepts. The law of non-contradiction can be understood as *preserving the meaning of "negation."*

Imagine we didn't grasp the concept of "false." Imagine that every proposition you'd ever heard was true, and every thought that ever crossed your mind was also true. You'd never encountered anything else. Now imagine you're talking with two friends. One of them says, "You have two parents." No problem. That's true.

Now your other friend says, "You have five parents." Wait a minute. What's going on? You'd never heard that type of claim before; it doesn't correspond to reality. What do you do? You have to develop a new type of concept: negation. You come up with the word "not." You say, "It is *not true* that I have five parents." The purpose of negation is to communicate an *explicit denial of the truth of something*.

Therefore, to negate and affirm something at the same time – to argue for a logical contradiction – is to misunderstand the meaning of "negation" and "affirmation." This is, essentially, the law of non-contradiction. Simply by understanding what we mean by our words, we can know that contradictions do not exist in reality. To say "X is true and not true at the same time" is to reveal a fundamental confusion about the meaning of the words "true" and "not true."

Negation also gives us the principle of "mutual exclusivity." Mutually exclusive things cannot be both true at the same time, as they would imply a contradiction. For example, "having two legs" and "having zero legs" are mutually exclusive. If you have two, you don't have zero, and vice-versa. Being "married" and being a "bachelor" are also mutually exclusive. Being "square" and being "circular" are mutually exclusive. Therefore, it's not an open question whether married bachelors or square circles exist.

They do not exist because they cannot exist, and anybody can understand why by grasping the meaning of the terms.

This is one demonstration of the power of logical reasoning. More will be explained in Chapter Four. When somebody makes an argument, and you can demonstrate that they contradict themselves, you can know that their argument is flawed. For example, when listening to political conversation, people often claim that taxation is a voluntary contribution to the government. However, by simply understanding the meaning of the terms "taxation" and "voluntary," it will reveal a logical contradiction. Taxes are, by definition, non-voluntary. Even if you enjoy paying them, you can't freely opt out.

When you start looking for logical contradictions in arguments, you will find them everywhere. This can be simultaneously exciting and frustrating for those who are interested in discovering the truth.

Inescapability

The laws of logic are necessary, universal, and *inescapable*. They cannot coherently be doubted, as they are presupposed by every idea, argument, and counter-argument. Even the most extreme skepticism cannot coherently doubt the laws of logic. To understand why, we need only examine the meaning of our words. What does it mean to be skeptical?

Skepticism is about being unsure whether an idea is true or false. It's about keeping an open mind and seeing the potential errors in any particular claim. It's about doubt. None of these things make sense without logic.

Packed into the meaning of "doubt" are the concepts of truth and falsehood. You cannot doubt something is true without presupposing the meaningfulness of "truth" and "falsehood" in the first place. You cannot have "truth" and "falsehood" without the laws of logic. You cannot coherently say, "I doubt that X is true" without meaning "I doubt that X is true" – implicitly accepting the laws of identity and non-contradiction. Indeed, even skeptical *thoughts* are bound by the laws of logic. Thinking "I am sure that X is true" is meaningfully different than thinking "I am *not* sure that X is true."

There is no coherent way to doubt the laws of identity and non-contradiction. By objecting to the laws, you've objected to them, which means your objections are whatever they are, and they aren't what they aren't. To make an argument without presupposing the law of identity is to make a contradictory argument that must refute itself. If it doesn't refute itself, it presupposes the law of identity. Since no coherent argument refutes itself, any argument denying the laws of logic is incoherent by definition. It's like somebody passionately arguing, "It is impossible for anybody to argue!" He is himself arguing, thereby refuting his own argument. It doesn't matter how passionately he insists nor the arguments he makes – he cannot coherently argue that he cannot argue. By engaging in any rational discourse, or by thinking any coherent thoughts, one is presupposing the laws of logic. Even without rationality at all, *simply by existing*, one is bound by the laws of logic, whether acknowledged or not. To exist is to exist. There is no way to exist without existing.

Therefore, skepticism, while essential to critical thinking, cannot consistently doubt an idea that it presupposes. Doubt makes no sense without truth. Truth makes no sense without logic. Doubt *appeals* to the laws of logic; it doesn't *apply* to them. I support doubting all ideas that can coherently be doubted, but that does not include ideas which can only be doubted by falling into incoherence. We cannot escape what is inescapable.

The laws of logic are the ultimate answer to "why?" questions. They do not require deeper explanation. They have no underlying cause. They are necessary. To ask, "Why are necessary things necessary?" is to reveal a lack of understanding about the meaning of the word "necessary." What is necessary is necessary – otherwise, it wouldn't be necessary. That's why we use the term.

The laws of logic, which are inseparable from all existence, are the root of every philosophical tree. They are the foundation of all knowledge. It's why I call them "square one." You cannot have any knowledge that is built on top of another foundation – as such knowledge would be self-contradictory and necessarily false. And, you cannot have any knowledge that is more fundamental than square one. There is no "square zero" – there is no deeper reason why logic is necessary.

No intellectual progress can be made, personally or in conversation, without agreeing to the laws of logic. You can only descend into incoherence and madness. The person who disagrees that "A is A" has rejected any possibility of making sense. No rational arguments could persuade somebody that "X is true" if they think that "X is true" is not meaningfully different than "X is false." Logic is the ultimate common ground for all arguments. Even if people disagree from square two onward, they must always be able to agree on the laws of identity and non-contradiction.

If you understand logic, you'll understand that I'll never be convinced otherwise. It's not dogmatism or pigheadedness. It's because in order for these ideas to be wrong, it requires them to be wrong – which would immediately imply that "wrong" and "not wrong" are meaningful categories, thereby presupposing the laws of logic.

The Law of the Excluded Middle

The laws of classical logic include more than just identity and non-contradiction. The third, more controversial law is the law of the excluded middle. It says that "propositions are either true or not true, without any third option." In abstract form, it looks like this:

(1) Either P or not-P.

So, we could say, "Either it is raining or it is not raining." Or, "Either Joe is a plumber or Joe is not a plumber." These claims seem certainly true. However, the universality of the law has been challenged by various schools of thought. Though it's not crucial to the claims in this book, it's worth understanding why people have objected. Take the proposition:

(2) The present king of France is bald.

Is that true or not true? Well, if we're speaking casually, it's kind of neither. It's certainly not "true" that the present king of France is bald – because there is no present king of France. But does that imply, "It is not true that the present king of France is bald"? Somebody might object to that proposition because it seems to imply that the present king of France has hair.

This type of claim in similar to the old question "Have you stopped beating your wife yet?" If you say "yes," then it implies you were previously beating her. If you say "no," then it implies you're still beating her. Either option, yes or no, contains a false premise. Therefore, some people have concluded that sentences like "The present king of France is bald" are neither true nor false. They do not have a truth value.

I disagree, though I can sympathize with the idea. Some propositions are so poorly constructed that to affirm or deny them implies more than intended. But that's because they are framed incorrectly. It is just a function of imprecise language and can be cleared up without much effort. To see the law of the excluded middle as universal, it helps to see claims as being bundled together with their presuppositions. So, "The present king of France is bald" actually contains multiple claims:

(2.1) There currently exists a king of France.
(2.2) He is bald.

Unless both of these are true, then "The present king of France is bald" is simply false.

Another reason to understand why the law of the excluded middle is universal is by thinking about the relationship between "truth" and "metaphysical reality." Things are true when they correspond to reality, and reality is not ambiguous. Reality is the way that it is. Therefore, claims either correspond to reality, or they do not. There isn't a third option.

Metaphysics

The most difficult and abstract feature of logic is its metaphysical status. What is logic *like*? Logic is not some spatially-existent object; you can't touch it. What *is* it?

It's a great question, and I can't precisely answer it. It's easier to first state what logic isn't. Logic is not a "thing." It isn't an entity within the universe. It isn't a "part" of the universe. You can't say, "Over here is logic, and over there is non-logic." Logic and existence are universally inseparable. Everywhere you point, there it will be. Logic does not have boundaries. There's no way to reference "it" as separate from something else.

Logic is the rules of existence. But what is the nature of a rule of existence? Metaphysically speaking, what *is* a rule? Here's where language starts breaking down. The word "rule" isn't quite precise. Usually, we think of rules as being "orders" or "instructions" – some kind of procedure to be followed. But logic is not a procedure. It's not in an instruction manual. You can acknowledge or disregard the rules in an instruction manual. Logical rules *must* be followed. They aren't optional. They literally cannot not be followed.

The entire universe is bound by the laws of logic, but not in the usual sense of the word "bound." Being bound by rules usually implies that "if you break these rules, you will be punished." But logical rules are not like that. They aren't some contract that you're supposed to follow. You don't have an option to follow the laws of logic. Nobody has to "enforce" the laws. There's no cosmic force making sure that squares aren't circles. It's not that "the laws are the way they are, but they could have been different." It's that "the laws couldn't be any other way." A law that couldn't be different does not to need to be enforced. The laws of logic are not in a rulebook. They aren't created by a rule-maker. They simply couldn't be otherwise. Not even an omnipotent God could break the laws of logic, because they are not something that can be broken. If a God exists, then he exists, and therefore he too is bound by the laws of logic.

Logic is something inherent to existence itself. The rules of existence are not able to be separated from existence. You could say, "For any thing that exists, there is some 'necessity' that is coupled to it – it necessarily exists and doesn't not exist." That *necessariness* is what you can call "logic."

So, to get as close to a metaphysical definition as I can: Logic is the self-identity of every thing. It's not a "feature" of existence. It's *the feature in every feature of existence*. Every part of existence is exactly the way it is – meaning logic is an inseparable part of it. You cannot separate the identity of something from itself.

Logic is not something which exists "in addition to everything else." Logic is part of the fabric of everything in existence. Without logic – without self-identity – you could not have anything at all.

Logic is not "the identity of every thing all together," as that would make logic everything, and it would imply that everything is the same. Logic is the *self*-identity of every thing. It is part of every thing, even if those things are different.

Non-Necessary Certainty

In addition to certain truth being known through logical necessity, there are other certain truths that can be known without logical necessity. For example, take the proposition:

(1) Awareness is a real phenomenon in the universe.

You could also rephrase this as, "Awareness is happening." This is a truth that can be known with certainty, although it's not logically necessary. We can imagine a universe existing without awareness going on.

Even if the *contents* of our awareness are illusions – if we're hallucinating – we can still know that the phenomenon of awareness is happening. To know it, we need only be aware of it. There is no argument that somebody could give that could convince me that awareness isn't happening. I have direct, certain insight into the matter. In fact, the certainty of the existence of awareness is more fundamental than the belief in the existence of a physical, external world. It's *impossible* for me to be wrong about my belief in the existence of awareness. It's *possible* for me to be wrong about the existence of an external world.

This might sound like Descartes' famous *cogito ergo sum* – "I think, therefore I am." However, it isn't quite the same. People have objected to the idea that an "I" exists. "I" implies a "self," and the self is notoriously hard to define. The existence of awareness avoids any difficulties with the self. Regardless of whether or not "I" exist, the phenomenon of awareness certainly does.

I can also be certain of the existence of the contents of my awareness. The experiences in my visual field, for example, are certainly happening. I see blue. Therefore, the awareness of blue – the feeling of seeing blue – is happening. This is true for all the contents of my awareness, whether visual, auditory, tactile, or anything else. It doesn't matter whether those experiences correlate to an external world. Even if I'm hallucinating, they still exist. Notice, this is a certain truth about metaphysics, which is often considered impossible to have in philosophy.

These arguments in Chapter Three should serve as a full refutation of all the arguments from implausibility. Humans can know certain truth, even if that seems peculiar.

Chapter Four:
Implication and Application

Conceptual Reasoning

Let's shift our focus from the logical structure of the world to the logical structures in our minds – our theories *about* the world. If we want to create theories that accurately describe reality, then those theories cannot contain contradictions, because reality cannot contain contradictions.

Theories are constructed out of concepts; concepts are referenced with words within a language; and those words have *meaning*. Conceptual reasoning is about unpacking the meaning and implication of our concepts to ensure that they are not contradictory.

Concepts are like individual pieces in a theoretical puzzle. The pieces need to fit together to create an accurate picture of reality. Conceptual reasoning is about analyzing, manipulating, and orienting the puzzle pieces in our mind. The shape of a conceptual puzzle piece is its *meaning*. Sometimes, two shapes don't fit together – when two concepts' meanings are mutually exclusive. The terms "married" and "bachelor," for example, have mutually exclusive meanings. You can't fit the pieces together in a coherent way. A "married bachelor" is a contradiction in terms and cannot reference anything in reality.

Our minds can use several powerful techniques in the realm of conceptual reasoning. In this chapter, I will cover three: presuppositional analysis, deduction, and propositional logic. These techniques are not esoteric philosophizing. They have immediate applications to the real world.

Presuppositional Analysis

As explained in Chapter One, ideas are not isolated from each other. They come bundled together. Presuppositional analysis is about seeing the additional concepts that come bundled with any particular idea. Those additional concepts are implicit, unspoken, and either *presupposed* or *implied*. For example, take the proposition:

(1) Jimmy broke the window.

If Jimmy broke the window, that *implies* that the window broke. If the window didn't break, then Jimmy didn't break it. This is a logical necessity.

If Jimmy broke the window, it *presupposes* that both Jimmy and the window existed. If Jimmy didn't exist, or if the window didn't exist, then Jimmy certainly did not break the window. This is also a logical necessity.

The distinction between presupposition and implication isn't important for the purpose of this book. The point is to demonstrate that some ideas are logically stuck together with other ideas. They come together as a package. By discovering and analyzing those additional, unspoken ideas, we can deeply scrutinize any theoretical claim about the world.

An excellent example of presuppositional analysis is a court trial. Imagine that Joe is accused of breaking into his neighbor's house and stealing his television. How can Joe prove his innocence? By presuppositional analysis and appealing to the laws of logic. For example, what is the *meaning* of the term "stealing"? What are the concepts that come bundled together? Stealing requires two parts:

(1) Taking somebody else's property,

(2) Without their consent.

Simply taking somebody's property doesn't qualify as stealing. Perhaps Joe was given the television. He can't steal something that was given to him. Theft requires a lack of consent. Joe can do a couple of things to demonstrate his innocence. He could object to prerequisite 1 or 2.

What if Joe proves that *he* was the original owner of the television, because his neighbor stole it from him the day before. In that case, Joe wasn't stealing; he was repossessing his own property. Or, Joe could demonstrate that he did have consent, by producing a contract that was written by Joe and his neighbor. Let's say they agreed to exchange goods. Joe gave his neighbor an old computer, and he got a television in return. If that's true, then Joe could not have stolen the television, because the concept of "stealing" *necessarily* implies "without consent." This isn't an empirical hypothesis. It's packed into the meaning of our terms.

We can analyze even deeper. What is implied by the concept of "taking somebody's television"? It implies physically being in some place at some time and taking an object from point A to point B. If Joe can prove that he wasn't in the correct physical location at the time of the theft, he can prove he didn't take the television. He could demonstrate that he was out of town when the theft occurred. If he was out of town, then he didn't steal the television. This is a necessary relationship between our concepts. *Alibis appeal to presuppositional analysis* – the meaning and implications of "doing X." This is true of any alibi. You can imagine a court defendant saying, "If I killed him/stole that/defrauded her, then P and Q would be true. Since P and Q are not true, I didn't do it!"

One more courtroom example. Say that a security camera recorded footage of the break-in. The tape clearly shows somebody other than Joe breaking in a taking the television. Why do we accept this as satisfactory evidence to prove Joe is innocent? It might seem like common sense – i.e. we can visually see that Joe wasn't the thief. However, the ultimate appeal isn't to common sense. It's an appeal to the law of identity. Joe is Joe; he isn't somebody else. If somebody else took the television, it couldn't have been Joe.

Take another scenario. Imagine you were to read a warning label on a new drug that said, "Caution: a recent study showed that 100% of patients died within two years of using this product." Sounds scary. The implicit message is, "Use caution, because this drug is extremely danger-ous." Most people probably wouldn't use such a product. However, the label might be misleading. It depends on the accuracy of the bundled presuppositions. Some presup-posed concepts:

(1) The study was unbiased.
(2) The study was conducted properly.
(3) The study included a representative sample of the population.

There are innumerable other presupposed and im-plied concepts. However, these three will demonstrate just how powerful conceptual reasoning is. If any of these presuppositions is false, then we've no reason to think the drug is dangerous. For example, let's say 1 is false. What if the study was conducted by a competing drug company that has a reputation for creating fake studies? That should cast doubt over whether or not to trust their conclusions.

Say presupposition 2 is false, and the study wasn't conducted properly. Perhaps the scientists involved were incompetent and had no clue how to create a trustworthy study. Perhaps they weren't even scientists, but a group of astrologers who divined their conclusions from the stars without actually going out and testing anything related to the drug. Were that true, their cautionary study would become irrelevant.

Say that presupposition 3 is false, and the study only included participants over the age of 95 with terminal cancer. Well, if that were true, then it wouldn't be so shocking that 100% of the drug's users died within two years.

These are only three presuppositions, and each one contains within itself innumerable other presuppositions. Whether or not the study was "unbiased," for example, depends on what concepts we mean by the term "unbiased." Even our conceptual explanation for what we mean by "unbiased" will itself contain more concepts, and so on.

When you intentionally seek out the presuppositions of any claim, it will greatly expand your knowledge and understanding of what's required to make a sound argument. You will see claims as bundled concepts, rather than isolated propositions. This, in turn, will lead towards greater skepticism, and you will quickly discover that most claims come packaged with concepts that are not well-justified.

Presuppositional analysis is also an improvable skill. If somebody is unaware of the bundled nature of concepts, they will have a difficult time seeing more than any immediate claim. However, over time, this ability can improve and become second nature.

Theory Versus Data

Conceptual examination also teaches us something about the relationship between theory and data. In the modern world, data is considered more important than theory. Our theories are supposed to play a supplementary role to the data we analyze. However, this is backward. Theory is inescapably prior to any interpretation of data. Data, by itself, is meaningless. It requires a theory in order to be understood. There is a popular notion that "data speaks for itself." It doesn't. For example, take the empirical claim:

(1) The more cops patrolling a neighborhood, the more crime recorded in that neighborhood.

Let's say the correlation is airtight – in every circumstance, we see a linear relationship between "the amount of cops" and "the amount of crime." What does this tell you? Not much. The data certainly doesn't speak for itself. Does it mean the cops are *causing* the crime, or does it mean the cops are *responding* to the crime? Without explaining the theoretical relationship between cops and crime, the data is perfectly ambiguous. Two different people, arguing completely different things, could both cite the same data in support of their theory. Even if they agree on the data, they must appeal to something else to make their case – namely, the theoretical relationship between their concepts.

More fundamentally, even *the process of gathering data* presupposes specific conceptual criteria. What qualifies as a crime? What qualifies as a cop? Does it include private police forces or only the public police? Does it include civilians patrolling their own neighbor-hoods? These are all conceptual criteria, prior to any analysis or gathering of data. If there are mistakes in our conceptual criteria, then there will be mistakes throughout the data. If somebody includes "kids dressed as cops" in their criteria for what qualifies as a "cop," then the data becomes poisoned. Before gathering any data, one must have concepts about the data being gathered. These are conceptual categories, meanings, and relationships that are all pre-empirical. They are purely theoretical.

Imagine I were to claim, "In order to be rich, you should go out and buy a Corvette. Studies have shown an extremely high correlation between 'being rich' and 'owning a Corvette'." To somebody with common sense, this is a ridiculous claim. But not because of the data involved. It's entirely because of our conceptual reasoning. The theoretical connection between Corvettes and wealth is not that Corvettes *cause* wealth. They are a symptom of wealth. What data am I referring to in order to back up my claims? None. I don't know any poor people who own Corvettes. I am relying on purely theoretical reasoning.

Now, it could be *possible* that purchasing a Corvette causes wealth. Imagine the following were true: in the manufacturing process of Corvettes, they secretly place $1 million of cash inside the glove compartment. In that case, buying a Corvette would indeed make you wealthy. However, that would also *change our concept of what a Corvette is*. If the concept of a Corvette changes, then its theoretical relationship to other concepts will also change.

This relationship between data and theory puts a damper on the extreme skepticism and empiricism of modern Western thought. We like to think that data speaks for itself and that our theories are only informed by empirical evidence. This is confused. Scientists might be *unaware* of their theoretical structures, but that doesn't mean they can escape them.

Our concepts structure all data that we receive. Data without theory is literally meaningless. Theory is what gives meaning to data. If we make incorrect conceptual categories about the world, it will result in inaccurate theories about the world, even if our data-gathering is precise.

A refutation of a theory does not need to come from empirical demonstration. It can come through purely conceptual analysis. Consider a popular idea proposed by Stephen Hawking. To paraphrase, he claims that "The universe can create itself out of nothing, because nothing turns out to have properties." This is conceptual confusion. "Nothing" cannot have properties, by virtue of what we mean by the term. If anything has properties, it is something and therefore not nothing. Hawking conflates "empty three-dimensional space" with "nothing." Empty three-dimensional space cannot be nothing, because it exists as something to reference. Perhaps empty three-dimensional space can create something, but it's not certainly "from nothing."

Theoretical critiques are far more powerful than empirical ones. It doesn't matter how much data Hawking gives to support his argument that nothing is something – he's wrong at a logical level. He cannot be right, because his conceptual categories contain a contradiction in meaning.

Deduction and Validity

Another powerful technique for conceptual reasoning is *deduction*. Deduction is a technique where you try to demonstrate that the conclusions of an argument *necessarily follow* from the premises. If you've constructed your deduction correctly, then it's considered to be a "valid" argument. If you've constructed your deduction incorrectly – if the conclusions do not necessarily follow from the premises – then it's considered an "invalid" argument. If an argument is valid, and its premises are true, then there is no way for the conclusion to be false. Consider this example:

(1) All men are mortal.

(2) Socrates is a man.

(3) Therefore, Socrates is mortal.

If 1 and 2 are true, then 3 necessarily follows. It is a valid argument. This is the straightforward goal of deductive reasoning. However, there's a deeper issue here. *Why* do such conclusions necessarily follow? Deductions have overwhelming persuasive power. But why?

It's a matter of logical necessity. It comes from identifying and preserving the meaning of our words. In the above example, the conclusion necessarily follows given the meaning of the words "all," "are," and "is." Even more fundamentally, it comes from the law of identity. We can see this more clearly by using abstract placeholders. Imagine the argument:

(1) All A's are B's.

(2) All B's are C's.

(3) Therefore, all A's are C's.

Again, the conclusion is necessary, given the meaning of the terms "all" and "are." This is a valid argument. If 1 and 2 are true, then 3 must also be true.

If we can clearly define our concepts and premises, then deductive reasoning can construct logically airtight theories about the world. It also helps us spot mistakes in reasoning. Imagine this argument instead:

(1) All men are mortal.

(2) Socrates is a man.

(3) Therefore, Socrates is *not* mortal.

Conclusion 3 obviously does not follow. It's an invalid argument. In this case, if the premises are true, then the conclusion is necessarily false, because it would imply a logical contradiction – Socrates being a man who is "mortal and not mortal."

Propositional Logic

Philosophers have created powerful techniques for analyzing the structure of more complex arguments to see if they are valid. It's called "propositional logic." Propositional logic is about breaking arguments into their individual components and analyzing the logical relationship between them. It can be understood as *preserving the meaning and implication of words like "or," "and," "if," and "then."* For example, take the horribly complex argument:

(1) If X is true, then either Y or Z is true.

(2) If A is true, then Z is not true.

(3) A is true.

(4) Therefore if X is true, Y is true.

(5) Y is not true.

(6) Therefore X is not true.

Is this a valid argument? At first glance, it might seem impossible to follow along. However, propositional logic contains tools to analyze whether or not the structure is valid. They are called "rules of inference," and they help you see the logical relationship between the propositions. In this case, the argument is valid. If the premises are true, the conclusion must be true. Depending on the source you read, there are anywhere from 10-30 different rules of inference, all of which are designed to preserve the law of identity and the meaning of our words.

Consider another example that uses natural language instead: If interest rates are raised, then the government won't be able to pay its bills. If the government can't pay its bills, then the economy will contract. But if interest rates are not raised, inflation will get worse. If inflation gets worse, the economy will contract. Therefore, the economy will contract.

Is this valid or invalid? Well, we can use propositional logic to break the argument into its abstract structure and see the relationship between the claims. It looks like this:

(1) If A, then B.

(2) If B, then C.

(3) If not-A, then D.

(4) If D, then C.

(5) Therefore, C.

This is a valid argument. It doesn't matter what the letters stand for. If the premises are true, the conclusion logically follows. Here's another way to understand the relationship of the propositions in the above argument:

(P) A or not-A is true.

(Q) Therefore, either B or D is true.

(R) If B or D is true, then C is true.

(S) Therefore, C must be true.

This is a valid structure of argument. Of course, valid arguments aren't all necessarily *true* – we could make a valid argument with ridiculous premises. I could say:

(F) If I went to the store, then I have carrots for fingers.

(G) I went to the store.

(H) Therefore, I have carrots for fingers.

This is a valid argument, but it has a false conclusion. That's because it contains the false premise F. Validity isn't about an argument being true; it's about the structure being constructed in a way where *if* the premises are true, *then* the conclusion must also be true. The error in the above example isn't because of the structure of the argument. It's the connection between "going to the store" and "having carrots for fingers."

A valid argument with true premises is considered a *sound* argument. Sound arguments are the ideal goal of critical reasoning.

Axiomatic-Deductive

A historically popular method for making sound arguments has fallen out of fashion in modern times. It's called "axiomatic-deductive reasoning." The point is to couple deductive reasoning with self-evidently true premises. The difficulty with deduction is finding true premises to start from. So if our premises are self-evidently true, then we're able to make sound arguments.

Axiomatic-deductive reasoning starts by finding an axiom – a truth that is either necessarily true or can reasonably be assumed as true. Then, you analyze that axiom to unpack the presuppositions and implications of it, building out a theory based on deductions. For example, an axiom in the philosophy of mind would be "awareness is happening." That is self-evidently true. I know it's true because I'm experiencing it. I can use conceptual analysis and deduction to figure out what necessarily follows from awareness happening.

An axiom in metaphysics and epistemology would be, "Logic and existence are inseparable." This book is an attempt to discover what necessarily follows from that truth. In economics, there's a branch of economic reasoning that treats the proposition "Humans act" as an axiom. Denying that humans act would itself be an action, therefore they take it as self-evident. What concepts are presupposed and implied by humans acting? Well, proponents of this method say that you can deduce truths about economic scarcity, choices, human preferences, and a lot more.

Axiomatic-deductive reasoning is about exploring the meaning and implications of concepts, and it's grounded in pure logical analysis. The danger is *thinking* that an axiom is self-evidently true while being mistaken. For example, nearly everybody assumes that "minds other than my own exist" and "there exists an external world." But these could be wrong. We can still build logically airtight theories around them – by *treating* them as axioms – but we must always keep open the possibility that they could be wrong.

At the beginning of this book, I said that if you build your worldview on sand, it will crumble. That's an understatement with axiomatic-deductive reasoning. If your starting axiom is false, your worldview won't simply collapse – it will explode into a ball of flames.

Certainty and the Mind

Take an example of axiomatic-deductive reasoning in the philosophy of mind. It's notoriously difficult to pin down what the mind is, but *the mere existence of certain truth* tells us something about the mind's nature.

The mind *must* have the ability to grasp objective truth. To state that "All things are what they are" is to make a claim about every existent thing in the universe, whether within our immediate awareness or not. This is an objective truth that we can know with certainty. Therefore, our minds must have some limited access to the so-called "God's eye perspective." We don't have to "get outside our own minds" to verify whether square circles exist in some part of the universe.

The mind is simultaneously able to state subjective truths and objective truths. For example, I can say, "Chopin is the best piano composer," and that is subjectively true. It's true for me, but it isn't necessarily true for anybody else. It's not "objectively true" in some cosmic sense. However, I can also say, "It is true that, in the universe, there exists at least one evaluation of Chopin as the best piano composer." This is an objective truth from the God's eye perspective. It's not just true for me; it's true for everybody everywhere.

Logic Games

Logic can also be used to construct systems. The rules of chess, for example, are logical constructions of our mind. We aren't metaphysically bound by the rules of chess. The rules of chess are metaphysically bound by us.

In chess, you cannot move the rook diagonally. It's against the rules. However, in some sense, you still *can* move the rook diagonally. You aren't physically restricted from picking up the piece and moving it to a new location. However, by doing so, you've broken the rules and are no longer playing chess.

Logical systems can be complete or incomplete, well-crafted or contradictory. Board games, card games, or even computer programming are all examples. A well-crafted card game will not allow for ambiguous or contradictory play. Imagine a board game where the rules read, "Whenever a piece gets placed on the board, it is immediately removed from the board. Whenever a piece gets removed from the board, it is immediately placed on the board."

That wouldn't be a very fun game. If you follow the logic of the rules, you'll end in a never-ending loop. The same is true of computer programs. Computer programs will break if their rules are contradictory. They can't execute what cannot be executed.

Constructed systems are constrained by the meaning of our words and rules. The popular puzzle Sudoku is a great example. Let's take a reduced version. Imagine I were to say, "Each number 1-9 is to be placed into a 3x3 grid." The grid currently contains the numbers 1, 2, 3, 4, 5, 6, 7, and 8. What's the missing number? The answer should be screaming in your head, "9!" Of course that's correct. But why?

It's a matter of necessity. Given the meaning of our terms in the construction of the system – by saying "each number 1-9 is to be placed into a 3x3 grid" – the missing number is necessarily a 9. It would be contradictory to say anything otherwise. Again, that doesn't mean you are metaphysically prevented from putting another number into the grid. But it means if you do so, you *cannot* fulfill the criteria set up by the construction of the game – you've lost the game of Sudoku.

Poker in Your Mind

Conceptual analysis isn't just useful for constructing theories. It also has broader implications for the old debate between "rationalists" and "empiricists." It helps to first give an overview of the two camps.

Roughly speaking, rationalists claim that some knowledge exists prior to any sensory data, and in some cases, theories can be known to be true despite empirical evidence to the contrary. Empiricists claim that knowledge is ultimately based on sensory information we gather about the world, and we must experience the world before we can understand it. To the empiricist, all claims about the world have to be tested to see whether they are true – our theories must conform to data we receive. It should not be surprising, given the preceding chapters, that I am a rationalist, although I think rationalists have to be extremely careful to avoid dogmatism. An excellent example comes from the game of poker.

Poker can be extraordinarily frustrating, because you can play perfect poker and still lose all your money. You can have a clear understanding of the game and lose to an unknowledgeable novice. The novice, by contrast, can play objectively horrible moves and yet walk away a winner.

So the question is this: How do you know when you understand the game of poker? Is when you start winning and get empirical validation that you're doing something right? Or, can you understand poker by manipulating concepts in your mind without any connection to real-world feedback? I say it's the latter.

Poker is fundamentally about probability – what the chances are that your opponent has a better hand than you, given the cards that you see and the psychological cues that you notice. What determines a strong hand from a weak one is *mathematics*. A strong hand will beat a weak hand the vast majority of the time. For example, say you're playing poker against one person, and the cards were just dealt. You have two aces, and your opponent has a 2 and 7 of different suits. With those cards, you've got about an 85% chance of beating him. Let's say he bluffs and bets all of his chips. The objectively correct thing to do is call him. However, he can still get lucky. If two 7's come down, he'll beat your aces with three of a kind.

Let's say it happened. You called him, but he got lucky and beat you. Frustrating, but not unheard of. Imagine it happens again. He keeps getting lucky, over and over. Instead of 85% odds, you get him to bet everything with 98% odds in your favor – total domination. But he gets lucky again and takes all of your money. In the world of poker, this kind of thing happens occasionally. Players tell stories of their so-called "bad beats," where they get terrible strings of bad luck, due to the inherent randomness in the game.

So, imagine after taking your money, your opponent says he's interested in understanding the game of poker, and he's a strict empiricist. You explain, "The reason you won isn't because you were playing better poker. In fact, I was outplaying you every hand. You simply got lucky. I can fully explain why your moves were incorrect."

He responds, "The data isn't on your side. Clearly, I kept winning, which means my moves were more correct than yours. If your theory were right, then you would have beaten me."

You respond, "No, my theory fully explains why you beat me. It isn't because you were playing better moves. I understand this *despite* losing all of my money to you."

He responds, "Why do you believe your theory? I am treating your claims as empirical hypotheses, and as such, all of the data contradicts you. Your theory should adjust accordingly."

This mimics the debate between rationalists and empiricists. The rationalists keep appealing to the logical relationships between their concepts. The empiricists keep appealing to the data. The rationalist won't be persuaded by more data, and the empiricist won't be persuaded by more theory.

Here's where the rationalists need to be careful. It's tempting to say, "There is no point at which I will abandon my theory, because I am appealing to the *logic* of the game!" This is the danger zone, because it's only partially true, and rationalists can slip into naive thinking.

Say that your friend keeps beating you, over and over, for years. The odds are always in your favor, yet he keeps winning. You could stick your head in the sand and say, "I cannot be wrong about my theory!" or you could look at the more plausible explanation: *the poker in your mind is not the poker you are playing*. Maybe you've incorrectly presupposed the truth of a variable. Maybe he's cheating.

There's an implicit assumption in the rationalist theory of poker that "the cards involved are the standard 52-card deck everybody is familiar with." What if that's incorrect? What if he's able to manipulate the cards in a way that breaks the presupposed randomness of the game? If he's cheating, or if you're using a deck of cards that isn't the one you assumed, then your theory is mistaken – or at least, your theory is about a different game of cards.

Rationalist theories might be internally consistent and beautiful, but who's to say whether they correspond to the world? If the rationalist is not open-minded enough to see alternative explanations and theories, then he'll never entertain the possibility that the conceptual scheme in his mind doesn't apply to the world. This is why rationalism and real-world feedback should be balanced with each other. Our theories might be airtight, but if the data overwhelmingly suggests we're wrong, it's a sign that our implicit presuppositions might be incorrect. We might perfectly understand poker, but that doesn't mean we're playing poker.

That being said, the most abstract rationalist theories about the world *cannot be wrong*. "Any thing is what it is" is a theoretical claim that will never be met with contradictory feedback, and it doesn't just apply to this universe. All possible universes are constrained by the same laws of logic, and I don't need to venture outside of this universe to know it. All metaphysical realms are metaphysical realms, and they exist in whatever state they are in. Therefore, the law of identity applies to them, too.

Hierarchy of Knowledge

The existence of foundational truth also implies the existence of a hierarchy of knowledge. Some ideas are categorically more important than others – those which are presupposed by a greater number of conclusions. For example, your beliefs about art history do not affect many conclusions. If you're mistaken about the works of Van

Gogh, it won't affect many other parts of your worldview. However, if you're mistaken about the law of non-contradiction, it might spill over into every part of your worldview. All ideas about Van Gogh presuppose the law of non-contradiction; the law of non-contradiction does not presuppose ideas about Van Gogh.

Philosophy, in general, is categorically more important than other areas of thought. Ideas about the nature of the world, the mind, perception, language, ethics, etc., are all presupposed by other disciplines. Conclusions from economics to English literature all presuppose philosophic ideas – while philosophic ideas do not presuppose conclusions in economics or English literature.

Pointing out this hierarchy makes people uncomfortable. There's a taboo against people speaking "outside their area of expertise." Philosophers are supposed to stick to philosophy, economists to economics, and physicists to physics. I think this is a mistake. Ideas do not need to be walled off from each other. In some circumstances, knowledge from one area of thought *should be* imported into other areas of thought. Political theory, for example, can be more accurate if informed by sound economic reasoning. Physics, in order to be sensible, must import concepts from philosophy.

In the modern world, the hierarchy of knowledge is often denied or structured incorrectly. People think that the natural sciences have the final say in any matter. This is mistaken, and a great example of it comes from quantum mechanics. It's become fashionable to argue that experiments in quantum physics have demonstrated that logical contradictions exist in the world. I will cover this in more detail in Chapter Five, but suffice to say, this idea is certainly false. Physics has nothing to say about the laws of logic.

Anybody is justified in commenting about quantum physics, even if they have no training in the subject, if it's being used to argue for logical contradictions. No empirical demonstration could ever disprove the laws of logic, as all empirical demonstrations *presuppose* the laws of logic. The only thing demonstrated by somebody declaring "Here is a true contradiction!" is that they don't understand the meaning of their words.

The hierarchy of knowledge is another way to understand the analogies in Chapter One – our worldviews are structured like trees, not spider webs. All ideas are not equally fallible and dispensable. Logic cannot be dispensed, as it is universally presupposed. All other knowledge grows out of the laws of logic.

Mathematics

Mathematical truths, if carefully constructed, can also be immune from the possibility of error. Logic is what gives mathematics its profound explanatory power. Propositions like "2 + 2 = 4" are not empirical hypotheses; they are logical necessities, given what we mean by the terms. They are certain truths, and they tell you something about the world. For example, take 1347 units of something away from 4192 units, and you'll be left with 2845 units. It doesn't matter what the units are – it could be distance, quantity, speed, etc. Mathematical truths apply to anything that can be quantified.

Some people try to deny the logical necessity of mathematics by giving examples like, "If you add one ball of clay to one ball of clay, you're still left with one ball of clay. Therefore, in some circumstance, one plus one equals one!" However, this is a simple confusion about language. It changes the units involved. It's saying, "One ball of clay plus one ball of clay equals one *larger* ball of clay." But that larger ball is twice the size of the smaller balls. It's saying, "1x + 1x = 1y." Therefore, 1y = 2x. No problem. Just by understanding the meaning of "one unit" of something, we can deduce the basic laws of mathematics.

There is much more to say about the use of logic in mathematics, but it's beyond the scope of this book. The connection between mathematics, logic, and the world is controversial and has been vigorously debated for the last century. In my own analysis, mathematics is simply an extension of logic. Therefore, the conclusions are necessary.

Paradoxes and Puzzles

The last implication of the laws of logic is about paradoxes. The modern intellectual sees paradoxes everywhere – inherent mysteries that can never be resolved the human mind. We're supposed to accept that some things are simply not sensible, and if the universe contradicts itself, so be it.

This idea is wrongheaded. There are no actual paradoxes in the world. All paradoxes are only *apparent* paradoxes and can be resolved with sufficient thinking. The universe cannot contradict itself, and if it ever appears that way, you can know additional thinking is required. I like to think of it this way: *everything makes sense*. Every part of the universe can be comprehended in at least the most abstract sense – everything is how it is, and it isn't how it isn't. Even if we know nothing else, we can still wrap our minds around the identity of every thing; it is as itself.

If humans can know something about every thing, then the universe is sensible in principle. This doesn't imply that we can possess all knowledge about the universe *at once*. Our brains aren't big enough. But it does imply that every part of the universe meets the most basic criteria for sensibility.

The Rubik's cube is a helpful analogy. When you first get a Rubik's cube, it starts in a solved state. Each color is isolated to its own side. After a minute of twisting, the cube becomes scrambled into a disorderly mess, and it becomes extraordinarily hard to solve if you don't know the correct technique.

Here's what's remarkable. If you know how to solve a Rubik's cube, it doesn't matter how long the cube has been scrambled; you can always solve it. There are about 43 quintillion possible combinations for the Rubik's cube, and each one can be solved in a matter of minutes – or seconds, if you're really good.

How do we know that a Rubik's cube can always be unscrambled if there are 43 quintillion possible arrangements? After all, it's not the case that every scramble has been solved before. The reason is because of *pure logic*. The scrambling and unscrambling of a Rubik's cube is essentially mathematics. We don't need to be empiricists about it. If you know that the cube started in a solved state, you can know with certainty that the end state will be solvable, even if the cube has been scrambled for a hundred years.

The Rubik's cube is analogous to the universe. Everything in existence starts in a solved state – every thing is how it is – and what appear to be paradoxes are merely scrambles of the cube. With careful reasoning, all the scrambles can be solved – i.e. all paradoxes can be resolved. Thinking that a "true paradox" exists is like thinking, "This scramble can never be solved! I've been scrambling it for so long that the cube is now beyond comprehension!"

The philosopher's job is to figure out how the cube works – to grasp the basic concepts involved in a paradox – and to sit down and unscramble things until they make sense again. Some paradoxes might take a while to resolve, but the philosopher has a cheat. He already knows the answer from the beginning: all paradoxes can be resolved. There's no worry that, "Perhaps *this time* we've discovered a true logical contradiction!" If it appears paradoxical, it must involve a conceptual or linguistic error.

Though understanding the laws of logic is sufficient to understand why paradoxes don't exist, there are many people who still object – those who are convinced they've found a real paradox. So, the next chapter will be devoted to refuting several arguments from impossibility – the idea that we cannot know certain knowledge *in principle*. If we can demonstrate an exception to the laws of logic, it would mean that the rules are not absolute and therefore are not foundational. Upon examination, nearly every objection to the laws of logic turns out to be confusion about the use of language or the meaning of words.

Chapter Five:
Objections and Paradoxes

The Liar's Paradox

The most popular paradox used when trying to demonstrate a "true contradiction" is the liar's paradox. Philosophers have been writing about it for thousands of years. It's supposed to be a proposition that is *true and false at the same time*, thereby demonstrating that the laws of logic are neither universal nor inescapable. If this is correct, then logic would not be a certain foundation for our worldview, and no such foundation could exist.

The liar's paradox can be formulated many ways. I will focus on one formulation, which I think ultimately resolves all the others. The paradox is:

(1) This sentence is false.

Think about it. Is that sentence true or false? If it's true that "this sentence is false," then it must actually be false. But if it's false that "this sentence is false," then it must actually be true. This presents us with a problem. If it's true, it's false, which means it's true, which means it's false, and so on. Thus, many philosophers have concluded that the liar's paradox is both true and false at the same time – a true contradiction.

Of course, given what we mean by "true" and "false," we can know that the liar's paradox must have a resolution. It's not an empirical question. Nothing can be both true and false at the same time – such an idea doesn't even make sense. So here's my preferred resolution to the paradox.

The liar's paradox is a linguistic error. It is not a meaningful proposition, though it appears to be at first glance. The problem is with the first two words: "this sentence."

"This sentence" is either impossible to define, or it's impossible to evaluate as true or false. To illustrate, let's begin by re-stating the paradox.

(1) This sentence is false.

One question gets at the heart of the issue: what *exactly* is false? In order to claim that something is false, we must know what we're evaluating. We need to know the precise function of the words "this sentence." There are two possible scenarios. "This sentence" could either be *a reference* to something, or it could be *what's being evaluated* as true or false. Both options turn out to be linguistic errors.

Let's look at the latter first. If "this sentence" is what's being evaluated as true or false, then we can quickly see the problem. "This sentence" simply isn't a truth claim. There's nothing to evaluate as true or false. It's just two words put next to each other. Imagine somebody came up to you and said only the words, "This sentence!" You wouldn't respond, "That's true!" That wouldn't make sense.

So in order to be sensible, "this sentence" must be referencing something. We again have two options. "This sentence" can either be referencing the entire liar's paradox or only part of it. In other words, the claim is either:

(1) "This sentence is false" is false. Or,
(2) "This sentence" is false.

Both options fall apart under scrutiny. The second option runs into the error mentioned previously. If "this sentence" is only referencing the words "this sentence," then it cannot be evaluated as true or false. "This sentence" is not a truth claim. Thus, the only attempt at creating a true contradiction must be formulating the liar's paradox as such:

(1) "This sentence is false" is false.

But this is merely one step removed from the original problem. What is the sentence being evaluated as true or false? If we're trying to evaluate the words in the quotation marks – "this sentence is false" – then we must ask the question, "What do the words 'this sentence' reference?"

If "this sentence" references only "this sentence," then as we established earlier, it's not a truth claim. But if "this sentence" references "this sentence is false," then the liar's paradox is *really* claiming:

(1) "'This sentence is false' is false" is false.

And we've gotten no further. This can continue ad infinitum. Every time you ask, "What exactly does 'this sentence' reference?" you're stuck with the impenetrable response "this sentence is false" or the non-evaluable "this sentence." It's like peeling back all the layers of an onion. Once you get to the true subject of the argument – something that isn't referencing something else – you're left only with the words "this sentence," which isn't anything meaningful to evaluate. Parentheses help illustrate more clearly. The liar's paradox is saying:

(1) Proposition X is false.

What is proposition X? It's "Proposition X is false." Therefore, the liar's paradox *really* formulated as:

(1) (Proposition X is false) is false.

Alright, it looks like we're a step closer. Now we have to evaluate the proposition within the parenthesis. Within the parenthesis, it's claiming "proposition X" is false. So what exactly is proposition X? It's "Proposition X is false." Therefore, the liar's paradox is *actually* saying:

(1)   [(Proposition X is false) is false] is false.

And again, we're no closer to finding a concrete proposition to evaluate. When "proposition X" references "proposition X is false," we're stuck generating an infinite regress. It continues:

(1)   {[(Proposition X is false) is false] is false} is false...

And so on. This is not a paradox. It isn't a true contradiction. It's simply a linguistic error. Some people will object to this resolution by claiming that we need to reformulate the paradox another way. Instead of saying, "This sentence is false," they will try:

(1)   The following sentence is true.
(2)   The previous sentence is false.

If you understand the laws of logic, you can know that this formulation must also fail. In this case, both sentence 1 and 2 fall into the same error as the original formulation. The same question illustrates it: what sentence *exactly* is true or false?

Examine the phrases "the following sentence" and "the previous sentence." Those phrases are either references to something, or they are what's being evaluated as true or false. If they are what's being evaluated, then it's clear they can't be true or false – "the following sentence" is as meaningful a proposition as "this sentence." It's just three words put together. It cannot be true or false. But, if "the following sentence" is a reference to something else, we run into the same infinite regress problem. Parentheses help illustrate:

(1) (The following sentence) is true.
(2) (The previous sentence) is false.

If "the following sentence" is a reference to something, then we could rephrase proposition 1 into:

(1) [(The previous sentence) is false] is true.

Now we must analyze the proposition within the parenthesis. What is "the previous sentence"? It's "The following sentence is true." So, the claim is actually:

(1) {[(The following sentence) is true] is false} is true...

And so on. Again, we've gotten no closer to a proposition to evaluate as true or false. If "the following sentence" and "the previous sentence" are references, then there will never be a truth claim being made. They are simply two phrases pointing to each other.

There are other ways to formulate the liar's paradox, and they all follow the same pattern. They appear to be sensible at first glance, but once you unpack the meaning of the terms, they are revealed to be linguistic errors.

The Bittersweet Paradox

Another popular argument for the existence of contradictions is what I call "the bittersweet paradox." It's another linguistic error. It goes like this: Contradictions not only exist; they can be *experienced*. Take two contradictory emotions like happiness and sadness. They are opposites, and yet we can feel happy and sad at the same time. The opposites can be unified into one experience.

For example, say that your mother recently died after battling cancer for years. Before her death, she was in agony from morning until night. That agony stopped once she died. How do you feel about her death? Well, on the one hand, you feel sad because your mother died. On the other hand, you feel happy because she isn't suffering. Therefore, you experience a contradictory state – happy and sad at the same time. Call it "happysad." It's as paradoxical as something being true and false at the same time. This argument can be broken up to see its core claims:

(1) Opposites are mutually exclusive.

(2) P and Q are opposites.

(3) P and Q are both true at the same time in situation X.

(4) Therefore, mutually exclusive things can be together.

(5) Therefore, contradictions exist.

Given the contradictory nature of this conclusion, we can know an error is nestled within the premises. In this case, as with the liar's paradox, the confusion is about language. The problem is with premises 1 and 3. With premise 1, the meanings of "opposite" and "mutually exclusive" are imprecise. With premise 3, it's not quite accurate to say "P and Q are both true at the same in situation X."

Let's start with premise 3. The "happysad" state isn't contradictory, because it's saying, "I feel happy about *one part of situation X*, and I feel sad about *a different part of situation X*." An actual contradiction would be to say, "I feel happy about one part of X, and it's not the case that I feel happy about *the same part* of X." That would be an affirmation and a negation at the same time, and it's obviously false. If you feel happy about one part of situation X, then you feel happy about that part of situation X.

The second problem is with premise 1. The terms "mutually exclusive" and "opposite" are imprecise. Mutual exclusivity is about a logical relationship between two things. It means "There is no possible way in which P and Q could be true at the same time." Two things "being opposite" is a much fuzzier claim. It's not clear what qualifies things as opposites, and it doesn't entail them being mutually exclusive. Consider the difference between these two examples:

(1a) I feel pain right now.
(2a) I feel pleasure right now.
(3a) I feel pain and pleasure right now.

Versus:

(1b) I have two legs right now.
(2b) I have no legs right now.
(3b) I have two legs and no legs right now.

In the first example, proposition 3a is possible. "Pain" and "pleasure" are commonly seen as opposites, but it's not difficult to imagine them being experienced together. They are not mutually exclusive. Most people don't feel pleasure when they feel pain, but some do. In the second example, proposition 3b is not possible. I cannot have "two legs and no legs" at the same time. "Having two legs" is logically incompatible with "having no legs." Putting those phrases together results in a contradiction.

Here's where the ambiguity of language trips people up. Though we might say, "having two legs" and "having no legs" are also "opposites," they are a different kind of opposite. They are *mutually exclusive opposites*, while pain and pleasure are not mutually exclusive opposites. The bittersweet paradox confuses the *appearance* of mutual exclusivity with *actual* mutual exclusivity.

Take another example. Imagine you entered a tournament and took first place. You also took last place, at the same time, in the same competition. Have you experienced a paradox? Of course not. There's at least one scenario in which no contradiction is present – if you were the only person in the tournament. Now usually, that doesn't happen. Usually, "being in first" and "being in last" are mutually exclusive. However, this isn't true in all circumstances. It would be a hasty mistake to think the laws of logic need revision because you experienced getting in first and last at the same time.

Simply by understanding the meaning and implication of our own concepts, we can know a certain truth: whether X and Y can exist at the same time is never a question of "whether mutually exclusive things can be together." It's always a question of, "whether two things are mutually exclusive." If two things are found together, they aren't mutually exclusive by definition.

The Logic of Nothing

My favorite attempt to incorporate contradictions into our worldview comes from a clever use of the term "nothing." Consider the sentence, "Logic applies to everything." That can be rephrased into, "Logic does not apply to nothing." If logic does not apply to nothing, then a skeptic might ask, *"What is nothing?"*

When talking about nothing, it's easy to fall into contradictions – by turning nothing into something. We have to be extremely careful in our use of language. After all, if we're talking about nothing, doesn't that mean were talking about something? How can we even talk about nothing?

This is another circumstance in which it becomes necessary to distinguish between concepts and their referents. The concept of nothing makes sense. "Actual nothing," as an existent thing, does not make sense. "Nothing" is a meaningful concept that can be understood as a *universal negation* – "not anything at all."

"Nothing," if meant as a metaphysical existent, is an incoherent term. Nothing cannot exist, because there's nothing *to* exist.

If I say, "There's nothing you can do to change my mind." That's saying, "There is not anything at all you can do to change my mind." It's not saying, "If you do something called 'nothing', it will change my mind." Nothing is not something that can be done. Therefore, there's only one sensible answer to the question, "What is nothing?"

Nothing is nothing. There is no such thing as "nothing" in existence. When we talk about "nothing," we're talking about the concept of universal negation. We aren't talking about an existent thing. Logic doesn't apply to nothing, but that's no exception to the laws, because nothing isn't anything.

Vagueness

Another objection comes from a criticism of logic being "too black and white." According to this argument, the world isn't so binary. Things are different shades of gray. Reality isn't as precise as we pretend it is. It's fundamentally fuzzy. Take the proposition:

(A) Joe is bald.

Seems like it's a black or white claim. Either he's bald or he's not bald. However, what if he's in the middle? Let's say he's got plenty of hair on the sides of his head but is balding on top. In that case, the question "Is Joe bald?" is too strict. We can't say yes or no confidently. He's half-bald. Even if he lost a few dozen hairs, he wouldn't really be bald, and even if he gained a few dozen, he wouldn't qualify as not-bald. So, is this an example of reality being fundamentally blurry – so blurry, that logic doesn't apply? Of course not.

This argument confuses the blurriness of language with the blurriness of the world. The world isn't ambiguous. Our language is ambiguous. When we use the term "bald," we're making a subjective evaluation in our minds. It's like saying, "The water in the bath is too cold." Our criteria for making that judgment are subjective and conceptual. At what point does the water in the bath become "too cold"? Whenever you think it's too cold. At what point does Joe become "bald"? Whenever you think he's bald. Joe has an objective, precise number of hairs on his head. Whether or not somebody references that as "bald" is irrelevant. The amount of hair is objective; the amount of "baldness" is subjective and arbitrary.

It's like the difference between the color red and the color pink. Imagine you're looking at a mixture of the two colors. What you see is not-quite-red and not-quite-pink. How do you answer the question, "Is this color red or pink?" You wouldn't respond, "It's red and pink at the same time because reality is contradictory!" You'd say, "It doesn't qualify as either. It's somewhere in the middle."

The spectrum between red and pink isn't a spectrum of metaphysical blurriness. Colors correspond to objective wavelengths of light. The wavelength isn't ambiguous; it is what it is. Once the light enters our eye, we have a subjective experience that we label as "seeing red" or "seeing pink." If some color doesn't qualify as red or pink, then you can give it a new label.

The same argument applies to other examples of vagueness. Say I'm standing half-way in a doorway. The front half of my body is in the room. The back half is outside the room. Therefore, somebody can claim, "I am half way in the room and not half way in the room at the same time!" But again, they would conflate ambiguous descriptions of reality with an ambiguous reality.

I am located precisely where I am located. Whether or not somebody wants to say I'm "in the room" or "out of the room" is entirely linguistic. If part of me is in the room, then part of me is in the room. If part of me is outside the room, then part of me is outside the room. These two descriptions are not mutually exclusive. Reality is not fuzzy, and neither is truth. A proposition cannot meaningfully be "half true," although we might use that term informally. For example, I could say:

(1) I am wearing two shoes and a top hat.

Colloquially, I could say this is "half true," because I am wearing two shoes but not a top hat. However, if we want to be precise, proposition 1 is simply false. It includes the word "and." Therefore, the claim involves three parts:

(1a) I am wearing two shoes.
(1b) I am wearing a top hat.
(1c) I am wearing them both at the same time.

All three of these claims must be true at the same time in order for proposition 1 to be true. Only proposition 1a is true, while 1b and 1c are false. Therefore, proposition 1 is simply false. Being "half true" does not make conceptual sense. It's simply shorthand to say, "Some of the criteria for this proposition to be true are met, while other criteria are not met." Each of those criteria is either true or false.

For the same reason, something cannot be "half-existent." Something either is, or it is not. If I say, "There exists a cat with black hair and an elephant snout," that is not referencing a half-existent. Some cats have black hair; no cats have elephant snouts. Therefore, no cats have black hair *and* elephant snouts. We wouldn't argue, "A cat with black hair and an elephant snout half-exists" because we saw a cat with black hair.

Universal Flux

Another objection goes like this: The law of identity is not absolute because things are in a constant state of flux. Things aren't "the way that they are" – they are in the process of "becoming the way that they are not." They are constantly changing. Nothing ever reaches a state of *being*, because it's always *becoming something else*. In a sense, things are strictly *not themselves*, because they aren't any particular way in the first place.

Take simple objects. What appear to be static things are actually a group of shifting and changing particles. The boundaries of physical objects are fuzzy and impermanent. The same is true for your own physical body. The cells are constantly dying and being replaced by new ones. At no point in time does "your body" exist – it's always morphing into a new assortment of cells. In this worldview, the only constant is the process of change. The world is in flux, and therefore, the law of identity doesn't apply to any thing.

This argument falls short, though it's a beautiful idea with proponents stretching back thousands of years. Embedded in these claims in a mistaken conception of "change" and "identity." The central idea is that constant change eliminates the possibility for identity. But this is backward. Constant change *presupposes* identity.

The concept of change has a logically necessary relationship with the concept of time. "Change" is another way to say, "At time 1, there existed situation X. At time 2, there existed situation Y. Situation X and Y are different, therefore the situation 'changed.'" Without temporal progression, change would be impossible and meaningless. Therefore, in order to have situation X in the first place – in order for it to change into situation Y – you have to have situation X in the first place. You have to have identity. In order for something to change, there has to be something.

If there is something, then it's in whatever state it's in. If it weren't in a state, it wouldn't *be*, and therefore it wouldn't change. You cannot have change without identity, because without identity, there would be nothing to change. You cannot have something exist in no state. Formally speaking:

(1) "To be in flux" implies "to be."
(2) "To be" implies existence.
(3) Existence implies identity.

"Change" presents no conceptual problem to the law of identity. Things do not have to be the same over time in order for them *to be*. Things can change over time, but at any given time, they are the way that they are. At any instant, there is no "change," because change requires temporal progression. In other words, the very concept of change presupposes the laws of logic. There can be no change without something being a particular way at a particular time. A changing state of reality presupposes a state of reality to change.

Eastern Mysticism

A similar idea comes from people importing Eastern philosophy into the West. I recognize that "Eastern philosophy" is a broad and imprecise term. However, there are distinct communication styles in Eastern philosophy that people use to defend the non-universality of logic.

Eastern writing contains many deliberate uses of paradox. Throughout Buddhist texts are cryptic questions like, "What did your face look like before your parents were born?", or the famous, "What is the sound of one hand clapping?" Superficially, these are logical contradictions. You cannot have one hand clapping, given what we mean by the term "clapping." However, when Westerners read this, they will often make one of two grave errors in response. They either:

(1) Reject the paradox as nonsensical and devoid of meaning. Or they,

(2) Accept the paradox as being a true contradiction that cannot be resolved.

Neither of these options is correct. The purpose of paradoxes in Eastern philosophy isn't to defend logical contradictions. The purpose is to get the reader to *find the resolution* to the paradox. You're supposed to read it in a non-literal way to find the deeper concepts that are meant to be communicated. To simply think, "I didn't have a face before I was born!" is to misunderstand the question.

In a nutshell, the central concept in Eastern teaching – speaking with broad brush strokes – is that our conceptions about the world mislead us. They are illusions created by our minds. Our minds divide up the world and place artificial boundaries in places that they aren't. Language fundamentally divides up reality into "this" and "that." However, reality itself is not divided. The mind deceives us about the true nature of the world.

To the Buddhist, truth is not something to be intellectually apprehended. The truth has to be experienced. When we're rationalizing things, we're caught in our own artificial constructions and concepts about the world. The Buddhist wants us to stop this concept-creation process and simply exist – to "quiet one's mind." This is the purpose of meditation – to stop the concept-generating process and try to experience the world without a filter.

Therefore, the cryptic paradoxes are not meant to be taken literally. They are meant to say, "Stop your regular thinking and grasp the bigger picture." The meaning of the question "What is the sound of one hand clapping?" is something like this: Your mind divides the world into multiple parts. "This" and "that," or "this hand" and "that hand." You do not realize that "this" and "that" are merely concepts. If you clap them together, they make a loud, distracting noises. If you didn't have the concepts to clap together, you might hear what reality actually sounds like. Stop dividing the world into multiple parts – quiet your clapping, your conceptualizing – and see what you experience.

That's a profound point packed into one cryptic question. Of course, I don't mean to imply that this is the only interpretation possible, but it's one way to resolve the apparent paradox. There's no logical contradiction present. All paradoxes are meant to do the same. You're supposed to find the resolution, not accept the paradox as true.

Another point about Eastern mysticism is the attempt to communicate the nature of "mystical experiences." People have claimed, for thousands of years, that they've experienced some state of mind that they describe as "being one with the universe," or "having the self become the not-self," or "being nothing." All of these sound like paradoxes, and we shouldn't take them literally.

I do not discount the profundity of mystical experiences. Many people say that their lives have changed because of them. However, what's going on is not logically contradictory. It's a demonstration of the limitations of language, not the limitations of logic. An essential part of the mystical experience is "ineffability" – it cannot be accurately communicated by language. When people try, they appear to contradict themselves. Not because the experience is contradictory, but because the nature of the experience cannot fully be expressed by language.

There's no conceptual difficulty with "ineffable knowledge." We have no reason to believe that all knowledge can be communicated by language. Some knowledge perhaps has to be experienced in order to be understood. Those experiences, however, also play by the laws of logic – they are however they are, and they aren't however they aren't. How something feels, that's how it feels, even if you cannot express it in words. If the literal interpretation of somebody's description of a mystical experience is logically contradictory, it's a mistake to either:

(1) Dismiss the experience as nonsense. Or,
(2) Accept that the experience was logically contradictory in nature.

The rational option is to grant the importance of the experience and recognize that language might not be able to communicate the knowledge precisely. The difficult job of the philosopher is to try to grasp and sort out the concepts being communicated in a non-literal way.

Quantum Physics

Another popular attempt to demonstrate a logical contradiction comes from appeals to quantum mechanics. People argue that "Quantum phenomena can be in two mutually exclusive states at the same time, demonstrating that the law of identity has exceptions." This argument, while fashionable, appeals to a flawed interpretation of quantum mechanics.

Obviously, the details of quantum physics are beyond the scope of this book. However, it's helpful to have a superficial overview of the subject – at least to show why logical contradictions aren't present.

We intuitively think that physics studies an external, independent world – that when we measure something, we're measuring some objective property that exists in the world. The police radar gun, for example, measures the speed of an independent thing, and even if we didn't measure it, that thing would still exist.

The standard interpretation of quantum physics challenges this intuition. It's called the "Copenhagen interpretation," and it claims that *there is no measurement-independent reality*. Particles, for example, do not have concrete positions until they are measured. An interesting question arises in the Copenhagen interpretation. What is the state of a particle *prior* to its measurement? According to the theory, a pre-measurement "particle" isn't really a particle. It isn't in one particular state. Rather, it's in multiple states at the same time – what physicists call a "superposition." Upon measurement, this superposition collapses, and the particle takes an actual, concrete position.

It's the concept of *superposition* that people appeal to when trying to demonstrate a logical contradiction. They think it means "something in two mutually exclusive states at the same time." This is a mistake. Quantum superposition *is not meant to be logically contradictory*.

Take a concrete example. Imagine that two people are making waves at opposite ends of a swimming pool. If they time their movement correctly, their waves will be in sync. When the two sets of waves meet in the middle of the pool, they will interfere with each other. If the peak of the wave in one direction is matched with the peak of the wave in the other direction, the wave will grow larger. If the peak of the wave in one direction is matched with the trough of the wave in the other direction, the waves will cancel each other out. When the two waves meet, the resulting wave – either larger in magnitude or smaller – is an example of superposition. The two different waves became "superposed" onto each other, creating a new state. There is no logical contradiction present.

Quantum superposition is different than regular wave superposition, but they are similar. With quantum superposition, the pre-measurement "states" are fundamentally probabilistic rather than concrete. Regardless, the point is that superposition does not mean "being in mutually exclusive states at the same time." The whole point of the concept of superposition is to claim that the states *are not* mutually exclusive.

That being said, I am not defending the Copenhagen interpretation. I think it's a terrible and unnecessary theory, with far superior alternatives available. However, in defense of the proponents of the Copenhagen interpretation, they would vehemently deny violating the laws of logic. Because of course, were it true that the Copenhagen interpretation violated the laws of logic, it would be a demonstration that the theory is false. A physicist cannot use physics to demonstrate a logical contradiction. Physics presupposes logic. A philosopher, however, can use logic to disprove a theory in physics – if the physicists are so naive as to accept logical contradictions into their theory.

The Unknown World

Another objection goes: There exists a physical world independent of our thoughts and language. We only gain conceptions about it by experiencing it. We can never know if it operates in a fundamentally logical way because we haven't experienced everything about it. Nature might be contradictory, but we simply haven't experienced it yet.

This is mistaken, given what we mean by "contradictory." It's true that we create concepts about a physical world based on our experiences, and those concepts might be completely wrong. However, even if all our conceptions about physics are wrong – let's say there is no "matter" or "energy" or "space" as we know it – the world would still be however it is, and it wouldn't be how it isn't. No matter how strange our experiences, they cannot be logically contradictory – an experience cannot both *have some quality* and *not have that quality* at the same time, given what we mean by the terms "and" and "not."

We can experience a *superficial* contradiction – a demonstration that our theories about the world are wrong. For example, two classical concepts in physics are "waves" and "particles." These are usually seen as mutually exclusive phenomena. When something is a wave, it isn't a particle, and when something is a particle, it isn't a wave. However, in quantum physics, experiments seem to show light existing as both waves and particles *at the same time*. Does that mean reality is contradictory? Of course not. It means our concepts are inaccurate.

As people experienced the world, they came up with a concept of a "particle," and they developed a theory about how they expected particles to behave. However, the actual phenomena in the world that we reference as "particles" behave differently than the theory predicts, and sometimes, those particles do things considered impossible by the theory. Does that mean "Something in the universe is doing something that it cannot do"? Of course not. That would be logically contradictory. If something in the universe is doing something, then it can do that thing. A demonstration of an incorrect theory is not a demonstration of a contradiction.

The physical world might be completely unknown to us. We might be constantly hallucinating about everything. However, even if we know nothing else about it, we can still know the most fundamental truth: it is however it is, and it isn't however it isn't. Statements about the world are still true or false – they either correspond to reality or they do not. If a theory claims that the world is in state X, but the world is actually not in state X, then that theory is incorrect. If the theory is incorrect, then it's impossible for it to be correct at the same time. That's what we mean by the words "correct" and "incorrect." Therefore, even an unknown physical world is still bound by the laws of logic.

That's Just Your Logic

Another common objection is to respond that, "That's just your logic! Other people have other logics!" Sometimes they will take the anthropological route and say, "That's just Western logic! Other cultures have other logics!" These objections view logic as a kind of human convention. Just like some people speak different languages, eat different food, and have different social norms, some people can have different logics, too.

This argument is mistaken, as should be evident by the preceding chapters. The laws of logic are not a convention. They aren't agreed to. They are inescapable. If people from different cultures exist, then they are bound by the same laws of logic. There is no "Western" or "Eastern" logic. It's all the same, universal logic.

The only "logical" rules that can be broken are within a constructed system, like chess. If you make an illegal move in chess, you're simply not playing by the rules of the game. It doesn't mean you've violated the rules of existence. You haven't somehow chosen to "be and not be" at the same time. If thinking of the rules of chess as being "logical" seems confusing, then label them as being "conceptual." Conceptual rules can be broken without existential contradiction.

Another source of confusion is people thinking that the rules of inference in propositional logic are followed "by convention." This is mistaken. The laws of propositional logic are all grounded in the laws of identity and non-contradiction. They are designed to preserve the meaning of terms like "if," "and," "or," and other connective words that express a logical relationship between multiple propositions.

Now, if somebody wanted to be pedantic and insist, "The *word* 'logic' means different things to different people!" then I concede that point. But it's irrelevant. The inescapable rules of existence bind everybody – whether or not you call them "logic" is beside the point.

Along these lines, some people take an extreme position and say, "Words do not mean anything at all, because there's no such thing as meaning!" But it doesn't take much imagination to see that this is a bad argument. You simply have to ask that person, "What do you mean by that?" By definition, words have meaning. Meaning is what differentiates arbitrary vocalizations from words. While it's true that people can make sounds with their vocal chords that don't have meaning – people can grunt – that doesn't imply that *all* sounds made with vocal chords do not have meaning. Such an argument is self-refuting, and it still presupposes the law of identity and non-contradiction. Different cultures might mean different things by their words, but they still mean something.

Different cultures do not appeal to different laws of arithmetic, either. "1 + 1 = 2" is a universal truth, regardless of the symbols you use to represent it.

It is true that people from different socio-economic backgrounds will *experience* the world differently. But that doesn't mean the fundamental structure of their experience is different or illogical. A Ugandan woman's life will be very different from a man's life in Sydney. However, their experiences share the same constraints – they are how they are, and they are not how they are not.

Mere Tautologies

There's a more traditional philosophic objection to the claim that logic represents the foundations of knowledge. People will say that "The ideas in Chapter Three are *mere tautologies!* They don't teach us anything about the world." In the modern vernacular, one of the quickest ways to dismiss an idea out of hand is to label it as "tautological," which is supposed to be synonymous with "trivial," "redundant," or "devoid of content."

To understand this objection, we first need to understand what a tautology is. A tautology is a proposition that is true in all possible circumstances. Sometimes people say they are "true by definition" or "self-evidently true." The central idea is that tautologies have no possibility of being false. Some people incorrectly call tautologies examples of "circular reasoning," but I will address that later.

The proposition, "All people with blond hair are people," is a tautology. It is true in all possible circumstances, given the meaning of our terms. The standard criticism of tautologies is to say *because* they are necessarily true, they do not add to our knowledge. They don't teach us anything we didn't already know. They are redundancies – mere word games – that do not even need to be stated.

These criticisms are wrong on all accounts. Tautologies are not only important; they are the foundations underlying any rational worldview. The law of identity is tautological and indispensable at the same time. There are three major reasons why tautologies should not be dismissed:

(1) Tautologies become important because people often deny their truth.

(2) Tautologies can teach us new information about the world, contrary to standard philosophic orthodoxy.

(3) Tautologies point to the fundamental rules of existence.

First of all, in a peculiar combination, some ideas will be dismissed as being tautological, while simultaneously being denied as true. People will argue that "things are what they are" is merely a tautology, yet in the next breath, they will argue that "things are what they are" is not universally true. You can't have it both ways. If tautologies are "trivially true," then they mustn't be denied. If they are denied, then they are obviously worth restating.

In some cases, this is because people conflate the idea of "validity" with "truth." They think that tautologies are valid-by-definition instead of true-by-definition. They conflate the *structure* of an argument with the *content* of an argument. Content is "what's being said." Structure is "how it's being said." The structure can be valid or invalid. The content cannot be valid or invalid. It is *true* or *not true* – it either corresponds to the world or it does not.

Validity is about the transmission of truth from premises to conclusions. It says nothing about whether a proposition is true in the first place. A valid argument says that *if* the premises are true, *then* the conclusions will be true. Tautologies, on the other hand, are propositions that are true themselves.

We can have tautological *forms* of argument that generate tautological propositions. For example, "A is A" will always generate true propositions regardless of what you substitute for A. It could be "dogs are dogs," or "things are things," etc. If we want to be precise, "A is A" isn't itself a true proposition (unless we're talking about the letter A). "A" is meant as an abstract placeholder for any thing. Regardless of what A is, it is itself. This tells us concrete truth about the world. It isn't simply a statement about the form of an argument.

In an ideal world, "things are things" might never need to be stated because it's self-evident. But that's not the world we live in, and swathes of people deny such truths. That's the reason for this book. Logically necessary propositions are foundational, tautological, and yet frequently denied as true.

Second, and even more heretical to modern philosophy, tautologies can actually teach us new things about the world. As I explained in Chapter Three, even an omnipotent God couldn't have created the laws of logic. Logic binds any omnipotent deities. This isn't a hypothesis. You can know it with certainty. It is discovered by unpacking the implications of the laws of identity and non-contradiction.

Growing up in a Christian Evangelical house, I know that a huge amount of people would disagree with this claim. They believe God created everything, including the laws of logic. They are mistaken. Ultimately, the reason is tautological, but it still tells you something new about the universe that you wouldn't know otherwise.

Consider an even larger set of truths: mathematics. Mathematics is fundamentally tautological. "2 + 2 = 4" is true in all possible circumstances. Yet, nobody would conclude, "Therefore mathematics is useless and doesn't tell you anything about the world." Math tells you all kinds of profound truths about the world, and few things are more concretely practical. This is because mathematical truths are fundamentally grounded in logical – tautological – reasoning.

Just because something is learned through purely logical reasoning doesn't mean that such knowledge is somehow irrelevant. The most important truths are those that cannot be wrong. Imagine an engineer who thought mathematics was filled with "mere tautologies." I don't think he's closer to truth because he keeps open the possibility that, "Some day we might discover that 2 + 2 = 5. We can never be sure."

Lastly, tautologies point to the most foundational ideas in philosophy. You simply have to ask *why* tautologies are necessarily true. The proposition "there exists no married bachelor" is a true statement about the world. Why? Ultimately, it's because of the rules of existence. Everything in the universe must be exactly the way that it is, and therefore, contradictions cannot exist.

I want to clarify one popular confusion about tautologies. Some people criticize tautologies as being examples of "circular reasoning." Colloquially, circular reasoning is where you assert your conclusion as a premise. For example:

(A)   Judy is the tallest girl in the class because she is the tallest girl in the class.

This proposition merely states its conclusion as a premise. To some, this might look like a tautology – "A because A." But crucially, this is not a tautology. There is an obvious circumstance in which the conclusion could be false: if Judy is not the tallest girl in the class. That possibility doesn't entail any logical contradiction. This is what differentiates circular reasoning from tautologies. Tautologies cannot be false without incorporating a contradiction. Contrast this to the proposition

(B)   All of the students in class are students.

This is a proper tautology; there's no possible circumstance in which it isn't true. Negating the conclusion would imply a contradiction – i.e. that "some of the students in class are not students."

So no, tautologies are not circular. They are simply true in all circumstances. Or you might say "they are not false in any circumstance." Being necessarily true is a poor reason to dismiss an idea as trivial or redundant. If the goal is to discover truth, it seems profoundly misguided to think that *certain* truths are the irrelevant ones.

Discovering tautologies is exciting, and it's synonymous with discovering truth. Any sound deductions that follow from a tautology must also be true. If we construct theories that are ultimately grounded in certain truth, we can build a robust worldview that is justified down to its foundations.

The Ultimate Resolution

Obviously, this chapter was not a comprehensive list of objections to the claims presented in Chapter Three. People are always looking for new ways to escape the laws of logic. However, though this book does not give specific responses to every objection, it does give the ultimate answer to every paradox: no matter what, it can be resolved. By understanding the laws of logic, you can know the answer to the question before it's even asked. Contradictions cannot exist in the world. We can be certain of it.

Logic represents the final answer to "why?" questions. It's the ultimate foundation that rests underneath all knowledge. Logic does not rest on any deeper foundation. It is necessary and universal. For anyone seeking the truth, I can think of nothing more important.

The Next Step

Square One is one piece of a theoretical puzzle. A robust worldview must contain more knowledge than epistemological knowledge. Logic tells us something profound in the abstract, but it doesn't tell us much in the concrete. This book doesn't answer many questions in metaphysics, the philosophy of mind, language, mathematics, religion, political theory, or ethics. *Square One* is the starting point, but it's not the ending point.

I am working on many other topics and intend to tie them together into one coherent whole. I am currently producing articles, videos, and a weekly podcast interviewing intellectuals from across the globe about these ideas. You can find them at *steve-patterson.com*.

If you value this project, then you can help support online. Since I work outside of academia, my work is funded by voluntary contributions by those who see its value. If you want to help contribute to the project, there are several ways you can support at *steve-patterson.com/support*.

I hope you found this book valuable. These ideas have changed my life and inspired me to continue seeking truth. I hope they do the same for you.

CPSIA information can be obtained
at www.ICGtesting.com
Printed in the USA
LVHW100905040922
727584LV00003B/238